THE
ASSURANCE
of SALVATION

THE
ASSURANCE
of SALVATION

Lam Cin Thang

*"If you do not know that you are saved,
how dare you go to sleep tonight?"*
(Charles H. Spurgeon)

XULON PRESS

Xulon Press
555 Winderley Pl, Suite 225
Maitland, FL 32751
407.339.4217
www.xulonpress.com

Xulon PRESS

© 2024 by Lam Cin Thang
Dimtak Lam
Manpi Fischer

All rights reserved solely by the author. The author guarantees all contents are original and do not infringe upon the legal rights of any other person or work. No part of this book may be reproduced in any form without the permission of the author.

Due to the changing nature of the Internet, if there are any web addresses, links, or URLs included in this manuscript, these may have been altered and may no longer be accessible. The views and opinions shared in this book belong solely to the author and do not necessarily reflect those of the publisher. The publisher therefore disclaims responsibility for the views or opinions expressed within the work.

Unless otherwise indicated, Scripture quotations taken from the New King James Version (NKJV). Copyright © 1982 by Thomas Nelson, Inc. Used by permission. All rights reserved.

Unless otherwise indicated, Scripture quotations taken from the Holy Bible, New International Version (NIV). Copyright © 1973, 1978, 1984, 2011 by Biblica, Inc.™. Used by permission. All rights reserved.

Unless otherwise indicated, Scripture quotations taken from the English Standard Version (ESV). Copyright © 2001 by Crossway, a publishing ministry of Good News Publishers. Used by permission. All rights reserved.

Paperback ISBN-13: 978-1-66289-971-3
Hard Cover ISBN-13: 978-1-66289-972-0
Ebook ISBN-13: 978-1-66289-973-7

CONTENTS

Preface xi
Foreword xiii
Introduction xv

PART ONE
THE WAY OF SALVATION

1. Sin 1
2. The Universality of Sin 4
3. The Consequences of Sin 6
3. Man Cannot Save Himself 9
4. The Penalty of Sin 12
6. The Forgiveness of Sin 15
7. Conversion 17
8. The Death of Jesus Christ 21
8. Redemption 23
10. The Blood of Jesus Christ 25
11. Eternal Life 30
12. The Gospel of Salvation 31
13. Peace 34
14. Propitiation 36
15. The Atonement 39
16. Reconciliation 41
17. Inheritance 43
18. Predestination 46
19. Union with Christ 49
20. Imputation 51
21. Justification 53
22. Sanctification 58
23. Justification and Sanctification 59
24. Glorification 62
25. The Last Things 65

26. The Life of Jesus Christ 70
27. Wonderful Exchange 74
28. How to Prove for Our Salvation 79
29. Eternal Security 81
30. When We Commit Sin, After Being Saved 93
31. Jesus – One Way 97
32. Old Testament People 101
33. Salvation and Rewards 104

PART TWO
COMPARE AND CONTRAST ASPECTS OF SALVATION

34. Salvation and Good Works 111
35. Relationship and Fellowship 112
36. Position and Practice 114
37. Law and Grace 117
38. Grace and Mercy 120
39. Two Garments 122
40. Two Grace 123
41. Two Births 125
42. Two Demands 126
43. Two Forgiveness 128
44. Two Relationships 130
45. Two Sons 133
46. Two Gates 134
47. Two Foundations 135
48. Two Kingdoms 137
49. Two Natures 139
50. Two Lords 141
51. Two Deaths 143
52. Two Resurrections 144
53. Two Destinations 146

PART THREE
EXAMINE SCRIPTURES RELATED TO SALVATION

54. The Noah's Ark 151
55. The Sacrifice of Isaac 154
56. Rebecca 156
57. Pass Over Lamb 158

58.	The Brazen Serpent	160
59.	Jonah	162
62.	Mephibosheth	164
61.	The Cities of Refuge	166
62.	Naaman	168
63.	The Floating Ax	170
64.	Joshua, the Priest	172
65.	Prophet Isaiah	173
66.	Salvation Made Plain and Simple	175
67.	The Roman Road Map	176
68.	A Justified Criminal	178
69.	The Holy Communion	181
70.	Conclusion	183
–	Prayer for Salvation	184
–	An Invitation	186
–	My Testimony	188

PREFACE

I am well pleased to be able to greet you all in the precious name of our Lord and Savior Jesus Christ. Grace to you and peace from God our Father and the Lord Jesus Christ.

It is with great joy and gratitude that I present to you this book that has been in the making for nearly five decades, which is a collection of materials that have profoundly impacted my life since I experienced the transformative power of being born again in 1975. These materials, sourced from various books and evangelists, have not only shaped my personal journey but have also been instrumental in my service to the church. As I reflect on the journey that led me to compile this material, I am filled with gratitude for the transformative power of faith. Since my spiritual rebirth, I have been fervently collecting these materials, driven by a deep desire to explore and understand the assurance of salvation.

For the past nearly five decades, I have had the privilege of sharing these materials in churches, Bible camps, crusades, and even during the forty-day Basic Evangelism and Mission Training at the esteemed Myanmar Baptist Convention. Additionally, they have been utilized in Language and Regional Groups across Myanmar, reaching countless individuals with the life-changing message of salvation. My passion for this subject has been further fueled by my years of preaching and teaching experience. Through countless sermons and lessons, I have witnessed the hunger and thirst in the hearts of believers and seekers alike, all yearning for the certainty of their salvation. It is this very quest for certainty that inspired me to compile the wisdom and insights shared in this book.

"The Assurance of Salvation" draws heavily from my previously published book on the same subject, originally written in Burmese. I have carefully selected chapters and refined the content to present a comprehensive and accessible guide to those seeking assurance in their faith journey. It is my hope that this translation will enable a wider audience to benefit from the insights contained within its pages. As we embark on this journey together, my heartfelt prayer is that the Lord will use this book as a powerful instrument in bringing back many lost souls to God. May its pages serve as a guiding light, illuminating the path toward a personal relationship with Christ, where they may truly know Him and be known by Him.

Why do I choose to publish "The Assurance of Salvation" in English? English serves as the official language for over 2 billion people globally, making it the most widely spoken language and a potent means of spreading the gospel. Additionally, many individuals who have migrated to English-speaking countries may not be proficient in our ethnic languages. Therefore, English is crucial for effectively conveying the message of salvation to them.

Furthermore, I hope and pray that ministers and laymen alike will find great value in utilizing this book as a tool for soul-winning. It is my sincere desire that as a result of their efforts, a mighty harvest will take place all over the world, ultimately preparing hearts for the glorious second coming of our Lord Jesus Christ. To God be the glory for the transformative work that has taken place through these materials. May this book serve as a beacon of hope, leading the way for the salvation of many lost souls. May its impact ripple across nations, bringing the light of Christ to the darkest corners of the earth… This book will tell you how to be 100% sure you are going to Heaven. Don't miss out.

In His Grace and Service,
Lam Cin Thang

FOREWORD

Rev. Lam Cin Thang has put together a very full and helpful book on the foundations of salvation and assurance. There is much to reflect on in the book. It will be helpful for new believers looking to establish their foundations, older believers who need a refreshment, those who seek to share their faith with others, and those who have not yet come to an understanding of Christian faith. In this book, there are many helpful expressions of what it means to become a Christian, walk as a Christian, and know the assurance God gives to his people that they are secure in Christ. There are very helpful reflections on the dual nature of many aspects of theology. This can be read devotionally or as a help to ministry.

I commend Rev. Lam Cin Thang on this work and celebrate its potential influence in building people up in the faith. As a local pastor, he knows how important right beliefs are in the lives of people. Our theology matters. It impacts our lives in so many ways.

This work can be read with confidence that the author has walked the walk and is very aware of the importance of being grounded on good foundations. I commend it to the potential reader as a faithful and helpful guide to the spiritual journey of following Christ.

Yours,
Rev. Dr. Mike Bullard
(Ministry Support Pastor Baptist Churches Western Australia)
21 August 2023.

The Assurance of Salvation

If you want to deepen your relationship with God and experience genuine spiritual transformation, I urge you to read the Assurance of Salvation by Rev. Lam Cin Thang, BA,BD, DMin. Dr. Lam has dedicated his life to living and sharing this message, having personally encountered our Lord Jesus Christ and accepted Him as his Savior and Lord while working as a senior high school teacher.

Despite facing poverty, sorrow, and happiness, Dr. Lam has continued to teach the Assurance of Salvation throughout Siyin Valley, Chin Hills, and to all ethnic nationalities nationwide as a resource person through Evangelism and the Mission of Myanmar Baptist Convention. His teachings are a testament to the transformative power of faith and the importance of glorifying God and edifying the church.

This Assurance of Salvation is a must-read for anyone seeking to experience God in their life and spiritual formation. It has impacted many ethnic nationalities worldwide, making it a compelling resource for anyone looking to deepen their faith, transform lives, and draw closer to God. Take advantage of this life-changing encounter with our Lord Jesus Christ. Read the Assurance of Salvation by Dr. Lam today.

Grace and Peace,

Rev. Thuam Cin Khai, EdD, PhD
Who's Who in America,
Who's Who Top Educators,
Military Chaplain, US Army Reserve,
Senior Pastor, Siyin Chin Baptist Church,
President, Judson Bible College & Seminary

INTRODUCTION

The assurance of salvation in Christ is a profound assurance that through faith in Jesus Christ, believers can have the confidence and certainty of their eternal relationship with God. This assurance is not based on personal achievements or merit but rests solely on the unchanging promises and grace of God. It is a topic that has brought comfort, hope, and encouragement to countless individuals throughout history, providing them with a firm foundation upon which to build their faith. Central to the assurance of salvation is the understanding that all human beings are inherently sinful and separated from God. The Scriptures teach that our sinfulness prevents us from reconciling ourselves with God through our own efforts. However, through God's great love for humanity, He sent His Son, Jesus Christ, into the world to provide a way for salvation. Through His sacrificial death and resurrection, Jesus offers forgiveness of sins and the gift of eternal life to all who believe in Him.

The assurance of salvation, therefore, stems from the unbreakable promises of God. Scripture assures us that those who genuinely trust in Jesus Christ as their Savior and Lord are forgiven, justified, and adopted as children of God. It is a secure and unshakable relationship, grounded in the unwavering faithfulness and grace of God. Ultimately, the assurance of salvation in Christ offers believers a firm foundation upon which to build their lives. It brings hope, peace, and joy in the knowledge that our eternal destiny is secure in the hands of a loving and faithful God. May this exploration serve as an encouragement and a source of guidance as we delve into the profound truth of the assurance of salvation in Christ.

The assurance of salvation in Christ is a profound and comforting truth that lies at the very core of the Christian faith. It is the unwavering confidence and certainty that believers have in their eternal relationship with God through Jesus Christ. This assurance is not based on our own merits but on the unchanging promises and grace of God. In a world where uncertainty and doubt abound, the assurance of salvation brings hope and security to the hearts of believers. It is an anchor that holds firm amidst the storms of life, providing solace and peace in the midst of trials and tribulations. Understanding and embracing this assurance is essential for every Christian's spiritual growth and well-being.

At its essence, the assurance of salvation rests on the redemptive work of Jesus Christ. Through His sacrificial death on the cross and His victorious resurrection, He secured forgiveness of sins and reconciliation between humanity and God. As believers place their faith in Christ, acknowledging Him as Lord and Savior, they are transformed and adopted into God's family, becoming heirs of eternal life.

Throughout history, theologians and believers have explored and articulated the various aspects of the assurance of salvation. From the doctrine of justification by faith to the indwelling presence of the Holy Spirit, different perspectives have contributed to a richer understanding of this profound truth. Yet, amidst the diversity of theological perspectives, the central message remains unchanged: the assurance of salvation is a gift from God, given to those who trust in Jesus Christ.

While the assurance of salvation is a gift that brings immense comfort, it is not a license to sin. Instead, it should lead to a life marked by gratitude, obedience, and a desire to reflect God's holiness. Misusing this assurance to justify sinful behavior is a grave error that contradicts the very nature of the Gospel and the transformative work of the Holy Spirit in a believer's life. Let us embrace the assurance of our salvation with a heart committed to living out our faith in purity and devotion. It is a call to pursue victorious life, grow in grace and love, and actively participate in the ongoing work of God's kingdom.

PART ONE

THE WAY OF SALVATION

1. SIN

In Christianity, sin is generally understood as a violation of God's will and a deviation from His moral standards. It is believed to be an inherent part of human nature, resulting from the disobedience of Adam and Eve in the garden of Eden, as described in the Bible. Sin separates humanity from God and disrupts the harmonious relationship between God and His creation. Sin is considered a universal problem, affecting every individual, and it is believed to have serious consequences for the individual and humanity as a whole.

The Origins of Sin

1. **Satan - Universe** (Isa. 14:12–15) Satan is often depicted as a powerful, rebellious angel who was cast out of heaven due to his pride and desire to be equal to or greater than God. He is seen as a tempter and deceiver, often associated with evil and the embodiment of sin. Satan tempted Adam and Eve to eat the forbidden fruit, leading to their fall from grace. The idea is that Lucifer, who was originally created as a magnificent and righteous angel, allowed pride to corrupt him, and he desired to usurp God's authority and be equal to or greater than God. This ambition led to his rebellion and subsequent expulsion from heaven, leading to his identity as Satan, the adversary of God, and the introduction of sin into the world.

2. **Adam - World** (Rom. 5:12) God created the first man, Adam, and placed him in the garden of Eden. God gave Adam and his wife, Eve, the commandment not to eat the fruit from the tree of the knowledge of good and evil. However, Adam and Eve disobeyed this command

and ate the forbidden fruit, which resulted in the fall of man. This act of disobedience is often considered the original sin, which introduced sin and its consequences into the world. The idea is that because Adam was the representative head of humanity, his sin corrupted human nature, and all his descendants (every human being) would inherit this sinful nature. As a result, all human beings are born with a tendency to sin and are spiritually separated from God from the moment of their conception.

Two Kinds of Sin

Sin is categorized into two main types: original sin and personal sins. Original sin refers to the inherited sin passed down from Adam and Eve to all of humanity. It is seen as the root cause of human inclination toward wrongdoing. Personal sins, on the other hand, refers to the individual acts or choices people make which go against God's will. Sin can lead to various negative outcomes, including spiritual death, broken relationships, and eternal separation from God.

1. **Original Sin** (Rom. 5:12, Ps. 51:5): "Therefore, just as through one man sin entered the world, and death through sin, and thus death spread to all men, because all sinned." Adam and Eve disobeyed God in the garden of Eden, they introduced sin into the world, and as a result, all of humanity inherited a sinful nature. This inherited sin is known as original sin. Humans are born with a natural inclination toward sin and separation from God. It is seen as a universal condition affecting all individuals from birth. It refers to that power within us that motivates us to commit sinful acts. It forces and compels us toward the way of lust and passion. It is related to our natural life.

2. **Personal or Actual Sins** (Mark 7:20–23): Personal sins refer to the specific actions or choices that individuals make, which are considered contrary to the moral teachings of the Bible. It is a passage where Jesus speaks about the things that defile a person, highlighting various sinful behaviors such as evil thoughts, sexual immorality, theft, murder, adultery, greed, deceit, and envy. Personal sins are seen as the result of individual free will and are considered offenses against God's moral

law. There are two kinds of personal sins. They refer to the particular individual sinful acts that we commit outwardly. They are related to our conduct and committed by the whole body.

1) Sins of Commission (Gal. 5:19–21): These are sins committed by actively engaging in prohibited actions or behaviors. Sins of commission include actions like sexual immorality, idolatry, hatred, rage, selfishness, drunkenness, and others listed in this passage. These are deliberate acts or choices that go against God's commandments and moral standards. For example, in Luke 10:30, the parable of the Good Samaritan begins with a man who was robbed, beaten, and left half-dead on the road. The thieves committed a sin of commission by actively engaging in theft and causing harm to another person. This act of violence and robbery is an example of a sin that violates the principles of love, compassion, and respect for others.

2) Sins of Omission (James 4:17): "Therefore, to him who knows to do good and does not do it, to him it is sin." These are sins committed by failing to do what is right or failing to fulfill one's moral responsibilities. Sins of omission occur when someone neglects to perform acts of kindness, love, mercy, or fails to fulfill their obligations toward God and others. In Luke 10:31–32, a priest and a Levite, both considered to be religious figures, passed by the wounded man without offering any help. They ignored the man's suffering and did not fulfill their moral duty to show compassion and care. Their sin was one of omission—a failure to act when they had the opportunity to do good. By neglecting the injured man, they violated the principle of loving one's neighbor and failed to fulfill their responsibilities as followers of God.

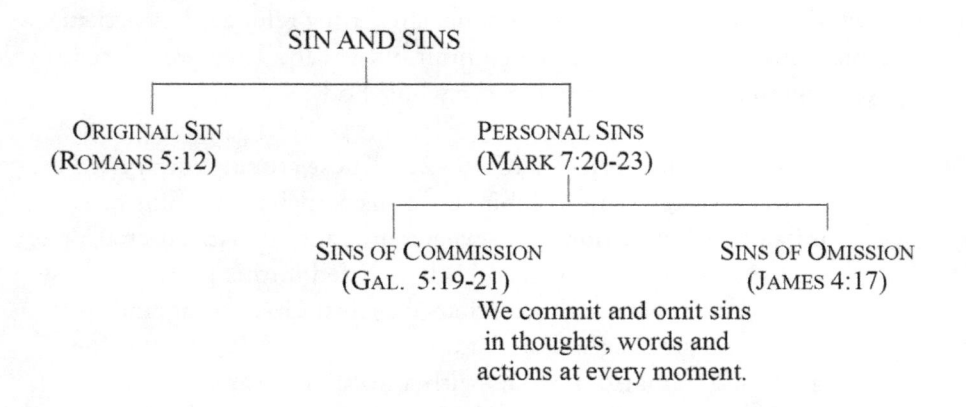

```
                        SIN AND SINS
                             |
        ┌────────────────────┴────────────────────┐
   ORIGINAL SIN                              PERSONAL SINS
   (ROMANS 5:12)                             (MARK 7:20-23)
                                                   |
                                  ┌────────────────┴────────────────┐
                          SINS OF COMMISSION              SINS OF OMISSION
                             (GAL. 5:19-21)                  (JAMES 4:17)
                                    We commit and omit sins
                                    in thoughts, words and
                                    actions at every moment.
```

In conclusion, sin represents a fundamental separation from God and His will, leading to spiritual, moral, and relational consequences. It distorts the human experience, bringing guilt, brokenness, and suffering. Without repentance and redemption, sin's impact can be eternal. However, through grace, mercy and forgiveness, the power of sin can be overcome, offering a path to restoration and reconciliation with God.

2. THE UNIVERSALITY OF SIN

In the Bible, sin is generally understood as any thought, word, action, or attitude that goes against the will of God or violates His commandments. The universality of sin refers to the belief that all human beings, regardless of their background or circumstances, are affected by and prone to sin. The Bible teaches that sin entered the world through the disobedience of Adam and Eve in the garden of Eden (Gen. 3). As a result, human nature became corrupted, and every person since then has inherited this sinful nature.

1. **Adam's Inherited Sin** (1 Cor. 15:22): As a result of Adam's disobedience, sin entered the world, and all humanity is considered to have inherited this sin nature from Adam. This inherited sin nature separates human beings from God and leads to physical and spiritual death. Therefore, "in Adam all die" refers to the universal human experience of mortality and the consequences of sin.

2. **No Difference** (Rom. 3:22b–23): The phrase "there is no difference between Jew and Gentile" refers to the fact that they are on

equal footing in terms of their need for salvation. It implies that no one group has a greater advantage or disadvantage in the eyes of God when it comes to attaining righteousness.

3. **Not A Just Man on Earth** (Eccles. 7:20): This verse acknowledges the universal reality that no human being is completely without sin or fault. It highlights the fallen nature of humanity, emphasizing that everyone falls short of perfection. It acknowledges that no one is perfectly righteous or without sin and the inherent flawed nature of human beings.

4. **None Who Does Good** (Ps. 14:2–4): In this Psalm, David expresses the observation that humanity, as a whole, has turned away from God and has become corrupted by sin. He asserts that there is no one who consistently does good, emphasizing the universal nature of human sinfulness. All humanity has fallen into a state of sin, and there is no one who consistently does good or lives in accordance with God's perfect standards.

5. **All Human Beings Are Born in Sin** (Ps. 51:5): This verse expresses humans are born with a sinful nature inherited from Adam and Eve's disobedience in the garden of Eden. It acknowledges the idea of original sin, suggesting that sinfulness is inherent in human beings from the moment of conception. The universality of sin underscores the need for salvation, and it highlights the equality of all human beings before God. It emphasizes that no one is exempt from sin or morally superior to others. This understanding promotes humility, as it reminds believers that they are all in need of God's mercy and grace.

6. **God Hates Sin**

   1) All who behave un-righteously are an abomination to the LORD (Deut. 25:16).
   2) But the things that David had done displeased the LORD (2 Sam. 11:27).
   3) You are not a God who takes pleasure in wickedness (Ps. 5:4).

4) Purer eyes than to behold evil, and cannot look on wickedness (Hab. 1:13).

The Bible teaches very clearly and very consistently that every human being is a sinner who has in some way fallen short of God's perfect standard of righteousness. Therefore, sin is a universal human problem, and every human being is in need of God's forgiveness and restoration. Without that forgiveness and restoration, all people, even those whom we would consider "good people," will one day enter the eternity of separation from God, an eternity of punishment for their sin. A sinner is said to be a sinner because he is born a sinner, not because he has committed sins.

3. THE CONSEQUENCES OF SIN

In the Bible, sin is often described as disobedience to God's commands or a transgression of His law. The consequences of sin are presented in various ways throughout the Bible, and they can be temporal and eternal. Here are some of the consequences of sin mentioned in the Bible: separation from God—sin creates a separation between human beings and God. In the book of Isaiah, it is stated that our sins have separated us from God (Isa. 59:2). Sin disrupts the intimate relationship that God desires to have with His creation.

BEFORE WE HAVE BEEN BORN AGAIN, WE ARE ...

1. **Dead** (Eph. 2:1): It begins with the assertion that we were "dead" in our trespasses and sins, highlighting the separation between humanity and God caused by our rebellion and disobedience. This spiritual death is not a physical death but a state of being separated from the life-giving presence of God. This spiritual death highlights the need for salvation and reconciliation through Jesus Christ.

2. **Children of Satan** (John 8:44): Jesus says, "You are of your father the devil." Before receiving Christ as his/her personal Savior, people are to be spiritually separated from God due to the original sin inherited from Adam and Eve. This separation is often seen as being under the influence of sin and under the domain of Satan, who is considered the adversary of God.

3. **Enemies of God** (Rom. 5:10): "For if when we were enemies . . ." People are separated from God and estranged from Him. It describes the state of being spiritually alienated or distant from God due to sinful behavior. In this sense, humans are enemies of God, not because God is inherently hostile toward them but because of their rebellion against God's ways. This rebellion against God's perfect and holy nature separates people from Him and hinders their ability to have a harmonious relationship with Him.

4. **Children of God's Wrath** (Eph. 2:3): "We all once conducted ourselves in the lusts of our flesh . . . and were by nature children of wrath, just as the others." He describes how people were spiritually dead due to their transgressions and sins, living in alignment with worldly and sinful ways before coming to faith in Jesus Christ. The phrase "children of wrath" suggests that, by nature, humans were deserving of God's wrath or judgment because of their sinful state.

5. **Condemned** (John 3:18): "He who believes in Him is not condemned, but he who does not believe is condemned already." Those who put their faith in him are saved from condemnation and receive eternal life. However, those who reject or do not believe in Jesus as the Son of God are already in a state of condemnation because they have not embraced the means of salvation provided by God. It serves as a call to faith and a reminder of the consequences of rejecting the salvation offered through God's Son.

6. **Cursed** (Gal. 3:10): "For as many as are of the works of the law are under the curse." Paul is addressing the issue of justification before God. He argues that those who rely on obeying the law to achieve righteousness are under a curse. This curse is associated with the fact that no one can perfectly obey every commandment of the law. Anyone who does not continue to do everything written in the Book of the Law is cursed (Deut. 27:26). The law sets a standard of perfection, and anyone who fails to meet that standard is considered cursed or under a curse.

7. **Prisoners** (Rom. 11:32 NLT): "For God has imprisoned everyone in disobedience so he could have mercy on everyone." In this verse,

the term "everyone" refers to both Jews and Gentiles, indicating that all people are held captive in a state of disobedience. Paul emphasized the universal need for God's mercy and grace. He conveyed that Jews and Gentiles, regardless of their background or religious status, are in need of God's redemption.

8. **Debtors** (Luke 7:42): "When they (2 debtors) had nothing with which to repay . . ." The Bible states that "all have sinned and fall short of the glory of God" (Rom. 3:23). Our actions, thoughts, and desires are tainted by sin, which means that even our best efforts are marred by imperfection. No amount of personal righteousness or good works can fully pay off the debt we owe to God. Therefore, humans, being fallible, cannot fully repay their debt of sin to God on our own.

9. **Sick** (Mark 2:17): Jesus says, "Those who are well have no need of a physician, but those who are sick." By comparing sinners to the sick, Jesus conveyed the idea that he came to bring spiritual healing and forgiveness to those who recognize their need for it. Just as a sick person seeks out a doctor for healing, sinners are the ones who acknowledge their need for salvation and repentance. Jesus's response challenged their self-righteousness and highlighted the importance of recognizing one's own sinfulness and need for God's grace.

10. **Lost** (Luke 15): All human beings are lost in Adam. Jesus used the parables to illustrate the concept of God's love, mercy, and the joy of repentance. These parables emphasize the message that God's love extends to all people, regardless of their sinfulness or mistakes. They demonstrate God's relentless pursuit of those who are lost, His willingness to forgive and restore them, and the immense joy in heaven when a sinner repents. The parables also encourage believers to have the same compassion and concern for those who are lost, seeking to lead them back to God through love, understanding, and patience.

11. **Foolish** (Matt. 7:26): "But everyone who hears these sayings of Mine, and does not do them, will be like a foolish man who built

his house on the sand." Jesus refers to the person who does not put His words into practice as a "foolish man" because they are making a poor decision that will ultimately lead to negative consequences. The analogy of building a house on sand signifies the lack of a solid foundation. When the storms come, such a house will not withstand the elements and will be destroyed (the Rock symbolizes Jesus Christ, while the sand represents acts of kindness and good deeds).

12. **Wretched, Miserable, Poor, Blind, Naked** (Rev. 3:17): The church in Laodicea was criticized for its self-perceived spiritual richness and material wealth. They believed they had everything they needed, yet they were unaware of their true spiritual condition. The phrase "wretched, miserable, poor, blind, and naked" is used metaphorically to describe their spiritual state. It emphasizes their need for spiritual growth, humility, and recognition of their dependence on God. The verse does not suggest that being physically or materially wretched, miserable, poor, blind, or naked is a requirement for salvation. It is highlighting the importance of recognizing one's spiritual poverty and need for salvation rather than relying on worldly wealth and self-sufficiency.

In conclusion, the consequences of sin are profound, leading to spiritual separation from God, inner conflict, and broken relationships. Sin not only disrupts personal peace but also creates distance from God, ultimately requiring redemption for restoration and transformation.

4. MAN CANNOT SAVE HIMSELF

According to Christian doctrine, humans are considered sinful and separated from God due to the effects of original sin inherited from Adam and Eve. As a result, humans are incapable of saving themselves and reconciling with God through their own efforts alone.

1. **Good Works Cannot Save** (Isa. 64:6): "But we are all like an unclean thing, and all our righteousness are like filthy rags." It acknowledges that all people have fallen short of perfection and are tainted by sin. The comparison of our righteous deeds to a filthy garment suggests

that even our best efforts to do good are still marred by imperfection and impurity. No matter how good our works may appear to others, they are ultimately insufficient to achieve salvation. Our inherent sinful nature prevents us from attaining the perfect righteousness required by a holy God. Salvation, therefore, cannot be earned through our own efforts.

2. **Law Cannot Save** (Rom. 3:20): "Therefore by the deeds of the law no flesh will be justified in His sight, for by the law is the knowledge of sin." It reveals the purpose of the law as a means to expose our sinfulness and make us aware of our need for salvation. It emphasizes that no one can be justified by works of the law. Humans are considered inherently sinful and unable to earn their salvation by following laws or performing good deeds alone. This sin separated humanity from God, making it impossible for humans to restore their relationship with God through their own efforts.

3. **Reformation Cannot Save** (Jer. 13:23): "Can the Ethiopian change his skin or the leopard its spots? Then may you also do good who are accustomed to do evil." Just as it is impossible for an Ethiopian to change the color of his skin or for a leopard to alter its spots, it is equally impossible for people who are deeply entrenched in a pattern of evil to start doing good. Similarly, no amount of personal reformation or self-improvement can fundamentally change the fallen nature of humanity. Our sinfulness goes beyond mere external actions and is deeply rooted in our hearts. Therefore, human efforts, including reformation, cannot bring about true salvation.

4. **Even Religion Cannot Save**

    1) Church Membership (Matt. 7:21): "Not everyone who says to Me, 'Lord, Lord,' shall enter the kingdom of heaven, but he who does the will of My Father in heaven." It teaches us that mere profession of faith or religious language is insufficient for entering the kingdom of heaven. True entry into God's kingdom comes through a transformed life or doing the will of the Father, that is to believe in him whom God sent (John 6:28–29).

2) Profession (Matt. 7:22–23): "Many will say to Me in that day, Lord, Lord, have we not prophesied in Your name, and cast out demons in your name, and done many wonders in Your name? And I will declare to them, 'I never know you, depart from Me, you who practice lawlessness.'" This passage serves as a cautionary message, reminding believers that outward expressions of faith are not sufficient if they are not accompanied by a sincere heart transformation. In other words, despite their religious activities and claims of association with Jesus, they did not have a genuine and deep personal relationship with him.

3) Religious Leader (John 3:3): "Most assuredly, I say to you, unless one is born again, he cannot see the kingdom of God." Jesus is explaining to a religious leader, namely Nicodemus, that it is not sufficient to merely follow religious laws or religious traditions. Instead, one must have a personal encounter with God, which results in a spiritual rebirth. This transformation is seen as necessary for a genuine relationship with God and for entering His kingdom.

4) Zeal for God (Rom. 10:2–3): "For I bear them witness that they have a zeal for God, but not according to knowledge. For they being ignorant of God's righteousness, and seeking to establish their own righteousness, have not submitted to the righteousness of God." The Jews have a zeal for God but are ignorant of the righteousness of God. Paul emphasizes the importance of knowledge and understanding in matters of faith. True righteousness is found in humbly submitting to God's righteousness and relying on His grace rather than attempting to establish our own righteousness through our works.

5) Giving (Ps. 49:7–8): "None of them can by any means redeem his brother, nor give to God a ransom for him—for the redemption of their souls is costly, and it shall cease forever." True redemption and salvation cannot be purchased with worldly riches, but they are available to all who turn to God with a humble and contrite heart. The psalmist invites us to shift our focus from the temporary and fleeting nature of wealth to the eternal and lasting value of a relationship with God.

6) Baptism (1 Cor. 1:14–17): "I thank God that I baptized none of you . . . for Christ did not send me to baptize, but to preach the gospel." Some Christians believe that baptism is essential for salvation and is the means by which one is cleansed of original sin or sins committed prior to baptism. It is often regarded as a symbol of one's faith in Jesus Christ and a public declaration of one's commitment to follow Him. Baptism is viewed as an outward sign or symbol of an inward change.

7) Holy Communion (1 Cor. 11:24–25): The act of participating in Holy Communion is not considered a means of obtaining salvation but rather a way for believers who have already accepted Jesus Christ as their Savior to remember and proclaim their faith. It serves as a remembrance of Jesus's redemptive work on the cross, His sacrificial death, and the forgiveness of sins that believers have received through Him. By participating in the elements of bread and wine, believers express their unity with Christ and with one another as members of the body of Christ.

In conclusion, man cannot save himself due to human shortcomings and limitations, such as spiritual death and moral imperfection, which prevent self-redemption. True salvation requires a power beyond human effort, often pointing to the necessity of divine intervention or grace for ultimate spiritual restoration.

5. THE PENALTY OF SIN

The Christian concept of the penalty of sin is rooted in the teachings of the Bible and the core beliefs of Christianity. Sin is understood as any thought, word, or action that deviates from God's perfect standards of righteousness and holiness. It is seen as a violation of the divine law and an offense against God's character. The penalty of sin, as understood within Christianity, is depicted as separation from God and the consequence of this separation. The Bible teaches that sin has temporal and eternal consequences. Temporally, sin can bring about various negative effects in an individual's life and in society, such as broken relationships, suffering, and

THE WAY OF SALVATION

the deterioration of moral values. However, the most significant consequence of sin is eternal separation from God, resulting in spiritual death and condemnation.

1. **How Terrible Is Hell?**
   The descriptions of various biblical references depict the nature of hell.

   1) Hell is portrayed as a place for the wicked, as mentioned in Psalm 9:17. It suggests that those who engage in evil deeds will be punished in the afterlife.

   2) The concept of flaming fire in 2 Thessalonians 1:8–9 symbolizes the intense and unrelenting nature of the punishment in hell.

   3) The term "torment" in Luke 16:23 implies the experience of great suffering and anguish for those in hell.

   4) Matthew 25:41 suggests that hell was originally prepared for the devil and his angels, indicating that it is a place of punishment for the rebellious and sinful.

   5) The phrase "everlasting punishment" in Matthew 25:46 suggests that the consequences of one's actions in life, rejecting Jesus, can have eternal implications in the afterlife.

   6) Mark 9:44 uses the imagery of a worm that does not die to convey the idea of an eternal state of suffering and decay in hell.

   7) Matthew 10:28 indicates that hell has the power to destroy the soul and body, emphasizing the severe consequences of one's actions.

   8) Isaiah 5:14 metaphorically describes hell as a place that opens its mouth beyond measure, implying its insatiable nature.

   9) Proverbs 27:20 states that hell is never full, suggesting that there is always room for more individuals to be punished.

10) "Weeping and gnashing of teeth" is a phrase used in Matthew 8:12 to depict the intense emotional and physical anguish experienced by those in hell.

11) Revelation 20:10 portrays hell as a place of fire and brimstone, emphasizing the imagery of destruction and punishment.

12) The "lake of fire" mentioned in Revelation 20:15 symbolizes the final destination of the wicked, representing the eternal nature of their punishment.

2. **Why Does the God of Love Send People to hell?** (2 Pet. 3:9)
   In 2 Peter 3:9, it is written, "The Lord is not slack concerning His promise, as some count slackness... but that all should come to repentance." This verse expresses the idea that God is patient and desires all people to repent and be saved rather than perish in hell. Hell is viewed as the consequence of rejecting or turning away from God's love and forgiveness. In this perspective, God's love is extended to all, but individuals have the freedom to accept or reject it. Hell is seen as the ultimate separation from God, a state that individuals choose by rejecting the love and grace offered to them.

3. **No One Escapes from Judgments:** (Amos 9:1–5)
   It focuses on the certainty and inescapability of God's judgment upon Israel. In this passage, God is depicted as standing by the altar, giving a command to strike the capitals and shatter them upon the heads of the people. The judgment described here is severe and portrays the inescapable nature of God's punishment. No matter where the people try to hide, whether it be in the depths of the earth, the heights of heaven, the top of Mount Carmel, or the depths of the sea, God will find them and bring judgment upon them.

The penalty of sin serves as a powerful reminder of the consequences of our actions and the potential for redemption. Through our spiritual journey, we witness the destructive nature of sin and the transformative power of forgiveness and self-reflection. As we navigate our own lives, may we heed the lessons learned from this tale and strive to choose path of righteousness and compassion, knowing that even in our darkest moments, there is always hope for redemption.

6. THE FORGIVENESS OF SIN

When Jesus Christ came into the world as a baby, Zacharias prophesied, saying "To give knowledge of salvation to His people by the remission of sins" (Luke 1:77). The ultimate goal of God's plan in Christ is to bring salvation to humanity. Salvation refers to the deliverance and rescue of individuals from the power and consequences of sin. It is the process through which people are reconciled with God and granted eternal life. "Remission of sin" means the cancelation or forgiveness of sins. The forgiveness of sins is a foundational concept in Christianity. Sin is understood as the rebellion against God's will and the breaking of His moral law. The forgiveness of sins is essential because it is sin that separates humanity from God, and forgiveness paves the way for reconciliation and restoration of the broken relationship between humans and God.

1. **The Needs:** At its core, the Christian understanding of forgiveness of sin recognizes that all human beings are prone to making mistakes and falling short of God's perfect standards. These shortcomings, known as sin, create a separation between humanity and its Creator. However, the Christian faith maintains that God, in His infinite love and mercy, has provided a way to bridge this gap through the forgiveness of sin.

2. **The Forgiveness of God:** The foundation of this forgiveness is found in the life, death, and resurrection of Jesus Christ. According to Christian belief, Jesus, being both fully God and fully human, lived a sinless life and willingly offered Himself as a sacrifice to atone for the sins of humanity. His death on the cross is seen as the ultimate act of love and a means to reconcile humanity with God. Through faith in Jesus Christ, Christians believe that they can experience the forgiveness of sin. By acknowledging their need for forgiveness, repenting of their sins, and placing their trust in Jesus's sacrificial death, they can find reconciliation with God and receive His forgiveness. This act of forgiveness is seen as a divine gift, not earned through human effort or merit but granted out of God's abundant grace.

3. **Forgive One Another**: The Christian concept of forgiveness of sin extends beyond a mere transaction or cancelation of wrongdoing. It encompasses a transformative process that brings about inner healing, restoration, and the opportunity for a renewed relationship with God. It offers believers the freedom to move forward, unburdened by the weight of guilt and shame, and the ability to live in accordance with God's will. Moreover, the Christian understanding of forgiveness of sin is not limited to the vertical relationship between individuals and God. It also emphasizes the importance of forgiveness among people, fostering reconciliation, and promoting harmony within human relationships. Just as God extends forgiveness to humanity, Christians are called to forgive others, mirroring God's boundless mercy and grace.

4. **The Trinity and the Forgiveness of Sin**

   1) God the Son
      a. Substitutionary death (Rom. 5:8)
      b. The cleansing blood (1 John 1:7b)
      c. The imputation of sin (Isa. 53:6)
      d. Paid all debts of sin (Col. 2:14)

   2) God the Father
      a. God will remember our sin no more (Heb. 10:17).
      b. Your sin shall be as white as snow (Isa. 1:18).
      c. God will cast all our sin into the sea (Mic. 7:19).
      d. God has cast all my sins behind His back (Isa. 38:17).

   3) God the Holy Spirit
      a. Convicting of sin and of righteousness (John 16:8)
      b. Seal and guarantee our inheritance (Eph. 1:13–14)
      c. Dwell in a believer (1 Cor. 3:16)
      d. To make a believer born again (John 3:3)

The forgiveness of sins is not universally applied to all humanity but is specifically offered to "His people," referring to those who put their faith and trust in Jesus Christ as their Lord and Savior. It is through faith in Jesus and acceptance of His atoning sacrifice that people can receive forgiveness and salvation. Through Jesus Christ, there is forgiveness of sins, and through this forgiveness, salvation is made available to those who believe. It emphasizes the importance of acknowledging our need for forgiveness, turning away from sin, and placing our trust in Christ's sacrifice for the remission of sins, leading to a restored relationship with God. This theme of forgiveness and salvation through Christ is woven throughout the New Testament and remains a fundamental aspect of Christian belief and theology.

7. CONVERSION

Repentance and faith represent essential steps in the journey of spiritual transformation and salvation for believers. These concepts are often intertwined, as they work together to bring individuals into salvation and a deeper relationship with God through Jesus Christ.

1. **The Definition:** "Conversion is our willing response to the gospel call, in which we sincerely repent of sins and place our trust in Christ for salvation" (Grudem 2022, 369).[1]

    1) Repentance: In Mark 1:15 and the teachings of Jesus, it refers to a sincere and radical change of heart and mind. It involves recognizing and acknowledging one's sins, shortcomings, and disobedience to God. The person who repents feels genuine remorse for their past actions and is willing to turn away from their sinful ways. It is not merely feeling sorry for one's sins but also taking steps to abandon a sinful lifestyle and strive for a new direction in life guided by God's principles. In the context of Romans 2:4, when someone truly comprehends the depth of God's kindness, patience, and mercy, as emphasized in the gospel, it can lead them to a genuine and heartfelt repentance. This repentance involves a change of heart, a turning away from sin, and a desire to live in obedience to God's will.

    2) Faith: Mark 1:15 refers to believing in the good news that Jesus proclaimed—the arrival of the kingdom of God. It involves trusting in God's promises and accepting Jesus Christ as the Savior and Lord. Faith is not merely intellectual assent but a deep conviction that leads to action. Through faith, individuals rely on Jesus for

forgiveness of sins and salvation, and they commit their lives to follow Him and His teachings.

3) Believe in His Person and His works:
   a. His Person involves His divinity, virgin birth, incarnation, holy life, resurrection, ascension, second coming, and His reign as King of kings, among other aspects.
   b. His Works include His substitutionary and redemptive death, His cleansing blood, His full atonement for sin on the cross, and more.

2. **The Relationship between Repentance and Faith:** In the Christian theology, the concepts of repentance and faith are closely related to the understanding of salvation and the Christian life. The apostle Paul says, "testifying to Jews, and also to Greeks, repentance toward God and faith toward our Lord Jesus Christ" (Acts 20:21). It highlights the relationship between faith and repentance.

3. **Salvation and Christian Living:** Saving (gospel) repentance and faith are once-for-all for salvation. However, it is important to note that they are ongoing processes in the life of a believer. It is the act of turning away from sin, acknowledging one's wrongdoing, and seeking forgiveness from God. It involves a change of heart, mind, and behavior. Faith, on the other hand, is placing trust and belief in God and His promises, particularly in the context of Christianity, trusting in Jesus Christ as Lord and Savior.

4. **The Need and Solution**
   1) Repentance:
      a. It recognizes the need for forgiveness and acknowledges one's separation from God.
      b. It involves a sincere desire to change and align oneself with God's will.
      c. It refers to the sincere turning away from sin and a genuine change of heart and mind.
      d. It involves acknowledging and confessing one's wrongdoing, feeling remorse.

e. It recognizes that all people have sinned and fallen short of God's perfect standard

f. Repentance prepares the heart, acknowledging the need for salvation.

2) Faith:
   a. It is through faith that we receive God's grace and forgiveness.
   b. It acknowledges our inability to save ourselves and relies on Jesus's sacrifice.
   c. It is through faith that we are justified before God and receive the gift of eternal life.
   d. It embraces the gospel and trusts in Christ for forgiveness and justification.

5. **They Are Inseparable**: Repentance (negative aspect) and faith (positive) are distinguishable but intertwined and inseparable. They are not isolated events that happen only at the point of conversion but continue to shape and transform the believer's life as they grow in their relationship with God. Genuine faith leads to repentance, as one recognizes the need for forgiveness and restoration through Christ. Likewise, true repentance is accompanied by faith, trusting that God is gracious and merciful to forgive sins through the work of Jesus Christ. It is important to note that while repentance and faith are crucial aspects of Christian salvation, they are not seen as works that earn salvation but rather as responses to God's grace. Salvation is a free gift from God, offered to all who repent and believe in Jesus Christ.

6. **Five Steps of Repentance and Faith**

   1) Conviction of Sin (John 16:8): The Holy Spirit's role in convicting individuals of sin is crucial for revealing their need for salvation and their separation from God due to sin. This conviction, prompted by an awareness of falling short of God's perfect standard, leads people to recognize the necessity of the sinless Savior, Jesus Christ. It emphasizes the impending judgment for sin and encourages

individuals to seek forgiveness, reconciliation, and hope in the gospel message.

2) Sorrow for Sin (2 Cor. 7:10): Godly sorrow, rooted in genuine remorse and acknowledgment of wrongdoing, leads to repentance and salvation. This deep sorrow arises from a profound understanding of the offense committed against God and others. In contrast, worldly sorrow is a superficial and temporary form of remorse, often focusing on the negative consequences of sin rather than the offense against God. Worldly sorrow may lead to despair or self-destructive behavior, ultimately resulting in spiritual death.

3) Forgiveness of Sin (Ephesians 1:7) underscores the Christian belief in redemption and forgiveness of sins through Jesus Christ. By His sacrificial death on the cross, believers are reconciled with God, and forgiveness is granted as an unearned gift through God's grace. This forgiveness is obtained by placing faith in Jesus and accepting him as Lord and Savior, symbolizing the removal of the separation caused by sin.

4) Forsaking of Sins (John 8:11) narrates Jesus's response to a woman caught in adultery, emphasizing mercy and urging her to "go and sin no more." This passage highlights the importance of forsaking sin, repentance, and the transformative power of forgiveness through faith in Jesus Christ. Forsaking sin is the result of salvation. It is the essence of Christian living. Because we have been forgiven, we are called to live as children of God. This revision clarifies the relationship between forgiveness and the Christian lifestyle.

5) Restitution for Sins (Luke 19:8) recounts Zacchaeus's repentance, where he pledges to give half of his possessions to the poor and repay fourfold to those he defrauded. This act of restitution, prompted by encountering Jesus, signifies the biblical principle that genuine remorse should be accompanied by tangible actions to rectify wrongs. Zacchaeus's commitment to making amends exemplifies the concept of restitution for sins, demonstrating a transformed heart and a desire for reconciliation and justice.

In summary, repentance and faith are essential for receiving salvation in Christianity. Salvation is a one-time event received through faith in Jesus Christ, not by works. However, the Christian life is an ongoing journey of growth, sanctification, and obedience to God, facilitated by the work of the Holy Spirit in the believer's life.

8. THE DEATH OF JESUS CHRIST

The understanding of the death of Christ as the substitute for sinners is a central concept in Christian theology known as substitutionary atonement. According to this belief, Jesus, through His death on the cross, took upon Himself the punishment that sinners deserved, thereby providing a way for humanity to be reconciled with God.

1. **Substitutionary Death** (Rom. 5:8): Substitutionary atonement is the belief that Jesus Christ took the place of humanity and bore the punishment for sin on their behalf. According to this view, human beings, being inherently sinful, are deserving of punishment, but Christ, who was sinless, willingly took upon Himself the penalty of sin in order to provide redemption. By dying in our place, Christ's sacrifice offers forgiveness and reconciliation with God.

2. **Vicarious Death** (John 11:50): Vicarious atonement emphasizes that Jesus Christ's death was not only substitutionary but also representative of all humanity. Christ, as the Son of God, acted as a representative for humanity, bearing the consequences of sin on their behalf. Through His death, He provided a means for humanity to be reconciled with God and receive salvation. This concept stresses the solidarity between Christ and humanity, as He experienced the consequences of sin to redeem all people.

3. **Redemptive Death** (Eph. 1:7): The death of Christ is often seen as an act of redemption. In Christian theology, redemption refers to the deliverance or liberation from sin and its consequences. Christ's death is viewed as the ultimate act of redemption because it pays the price for humanity's sins and provides the opportunity for individuals to be redeemed and restored to a right relationship with God.

4. **Propitiatory Death** (1 John 2:2): Propitiation refers to the act of appeasing or satisfying a deity's wrath or justice. In Christian theology, it is believed that all people have sinned and fallen short of God's perfect standard. The death of Christ is seen as a propitiation or atoning sacrifice, satisfying God's justice and wrath against sin. Through his sacrificial death, Christ bears the punishment that humanity deserves, allowing believers to be reconciled to God and receive forgiveness.

5. **Death of Reconciliation** (2 Cor. 5:18–19): All humans are separated from God due to sin, which is a state of spiritual brokenness and rebellion against God's perfect standards. Sin creates a barrier between humanity and God, preventing a harmonious relationship. In the death of reconciliation, Jesus willingly sacrificed Himself as an atoning sacrifice to bridge this gap caused by sin. He took upon Himself the punishment that humanity deserved, thereby satisfying God's justice. Through His death, Jesus offers forgiveness and reconciliation to all who accept Him as Lord and Savior.

6. **Death of Imputation** (2 Cor. 5:21): The Death of Imputation refers to the belief that through His death, Jesus bore the sins of humanity and imputed His righteousness to believers. Imputation means to attribute or assign something to someone else's account. In the death of imputation, believers are considered to be "in Christ." Their sins are imputed to Jesus, and His righteousness is imputed to them. This imputation allows believers to be reconciled to God, not based on their own merit or actions but solely on the merit of Christ.

7. **Death of Sanctification** (Heb. 10:10): Sanctification refers to the process of being made holy or set apart for God's purposes. The death of Christ supersedes those Old Testament sacrifices because Jesus, as the perfect and sinless Son of God, offered Himself as the ultimate sacrifice for the forgiveness of sins. Through His death, Jesus sanctified believers by providing them with a means to be cleansed from sin and reconciled with God. His sacrifice is considered sufficient and once-for-all, meaning that it does not need to be repeated.

8. **Death of Perfection** (Heb. 10:14): Perfection, in this context, does not refer to flawlessness in a human sense but rather to completeness

and wholeness. The death of Christ is seen as the ultimate sacrifice that accomplishes what previous sacrifices could not achieve. It provides a way for humans to be reconciled with God and obtain salvation. Through Christ's sacrifice, believers are made perfect forever. This means that the work of Christ on the cross is complete and final, and it secures eternal salvation for those who trust in Him. It is not a temporary or partial solution but an all-encompassing act that brings about the fullness of redemption.

9. **Death of Shame** (Heb. 12:2): The interpretation suggests that through Jesus's sacrificial death on the cross, believers are delivered from eternal shame. This concept aligns with Christian theology, which teaches that Jesus's death and resurrection provide redemption and forgiveness for humanity's sins, offering believers the opportunity to have eternal life and be reconciled with God. The idea is that Jesus's willingness to bear the shame of the crucifixion serves as a means of deliverance from the shame and guilt of sin that humanity experiences. By embracing faith in Jesus and his sacrifice, believers can find spiritual freedom and hope, ultimately avoiding the eternal shame that might be associated with their sins.

Through Jesus's death, the penalty for human sin was fully paid, and the righteousness of God was upheld. As a result, those who place their faith in Jesus and accept his sacrifice are forgiven of their sins and reconciled with God.

9. REDEMPTION

The Christian concept of redemption is a fundamental and central theme within Christian theology, emphasizing the idea of salvation and deliverance from sin. Rooted in the belief that humanity is inherently sinful, redemption is seen as the process by which individuals can be reconciled with God through the atoning sacrifice of Jesus Christ. This concept underscores the transformative power of faith, highlighting the idea that through acceptance of Christ's sacrifice, believers can experience forgiveness, restoration, and a renewed relationship with God. The Christian understanding of redemption not only addresses the consequences of sin but also offers a path towards spiritual renewal and eternal life. This profound concept resonates throughout Christian teachings, shaping the core beliefs and practices of the faith.

> Grudem defines that "We as sinners are in bondage to sin and to Satan, we need someone to provide redemption and thereby 'redeem' us out of that bondage. When we speak of redemption, the idea of a 'ransom' comes into view. A ransom is the price paid to redeem someone from bondage or captivity" (Grudem 1994, 580).[2]

1. **The Problem of Sin:** From the Christian standpoint, sin refers to the violation of God's will. The Bible explains that God created humankind free of evil, but they tainted themselves when Adam and Eve committed the original sin. Consequently, humans are born sinners to live in a world characterized by sins and temptation. Romans 3:23 states that every person has sinned and fallen short of God's glorious standard.

2. **Jesus Secured an Eternal Redemption for Us:** The animal sacrifice of the Old Testament provided a temporal covering for sin but could never take away sin. Jesus, however, is the Lamb of God who takes away the sin of the world. Because Jesus's single sacrifice was perfect, it secured an eternal redemption for the humanity. This means that anyone who receives Jesus by grace alone, through faith alone, will enjoy the benefits of His redemption forever. His blood cleanses us from all our sins. And by it, we can enter the holy places of heaven with full confidence and assurance (Heb. 9:11–12, 14–15, 25–26; 10:19–22; John 1:29; 1 John 1:7–9).

3. **The Benefits of Jesus's Redemption:** Jesus has redeemed Christians from lawlessness, that is, our sins, and the curse of the law, which is the task of obtaining righteousness through perfectly obeying God's law, which no one but Jesus has done. We are justified by grace through faith alone because of Jesus's redemption. His redemption was what made salvation possible to begin with. Jesus acted as our substitute by offering His own perfect and sinless life on the cross as the price that sets believers free from all their sins, the power of death, and the devil (Titus 2:13–14; Gal. 3:13–14; Rom. 3:23–25; Heb. 2:14–15).

Through his death and resurrection, Jesus has conquered sin and death, offering eternal life to those who believe in him and accept his gift of salvation. Christians believe that by placing their faith in Jesus, acknowledging him as their Lord and Savior, and repenting of their sins, they can be forgiven and reconciled with God. The redemption Jesus brought is considered a central and foundational aspect of Christian belief. It is believed to offer liberation from the bondage of sin, the assurance of God's love and forgiveness, and the promise of eternal life with God. The redemption of Jesus Christ is a cornerstone of Christian faith and serves as a source of hope, comfort, and transformation for believers.

10. THE BLOOD OF JESUS CHRIST

In Christian doctrine, sin is seen as a separation from God, with death as its consequence. Jesus's sacrificial death, symbolized by the shedding of his blood, is central to Christian beliefs, offering forgiveness and redemption. His blood is considered powerful, cleansing believers from sin and reconciling them with God. Salvation, the deliverance from sin's consequences, is achieved through Jesus's atoning sacrifice. Christians believe Jesus willingly shed his blood on the cross, paying the price for humanity's sins. This act is regarded as the ultimate expression of God's grace and mercy, emphasizing the restoration of the relationship between believers and God.

1. **The Life-Giving Blood** (Lev. 17:11): This verse highlights the significance of blood in making atonement for one's life. In the context of Christianity, the shedding of Jesus's blood is often interpreted as a sacrificial act to bring about atonement and forgiveness of sins. It states that the life of a creature resides in its blood, and God has designated blood as the means of atonement for human life. In this context, atonement refers to the process of seeking forgiveness and reconciliation with God for sins committed.

2. **The Blood of Passover** (Exod. 12:13): When the Israelites were preparing to leave Egypt, God commanded them to sacrifice a lamb and mark their doorposts with its blood. The blood served as a sign for the angel of death to "pass over" those households and spare their firstborn from the final plague that struck Egypt. The blood acted as a sign to spare them from the final plague. This event foreshadows the sacrifice

of Jesus as the Lamb of God, whose blood brings deliverance and salvation (1 Cor. 5:7).

3. **The Blood of Remission** (Eph. 1:7): It emphasizes that believers find forgiveness and freedom from the consequences of sin through Jesus's sacrificial death. It is based on the belief that Jesus's sacrificial death provides redemption and atonement for humanity's sins. According to this view, the shedding of Jesus's blood is seen as a necessary act for the remission, or forgiveness, of sins.

4. **The Blood of Redemption** (1 Pet. 1:18–19): This passage speaks of the preciousness and efficacy of Jesus's blood as the means of redemption. This highlights the incomparable value of Jesus's sacrifice, contrasting it with worldly wealth that is fleeting and temporary. The shedding of Jesus's blood represents the ultimate act of selfless love and atonement, making it possible for humanity to be reconciled with God.

5. **The Blood of Reconciliation** (Col. 1:20): The blood of Christ is seen here as instrumental in reconciling all things to God, bringing about peace. The concept of reconciliation, the restoration of a harmonious relationship between God and humanity. Through Jesus's sacrificial death, the separation caused by sin is overcome, and a reconciliation between God and humanity is made possible. The blood of Jesus is seen as the means by which this reconciliation is achieved, as it symbolizes the complete offering of Jesus's life and the bridge that brings humanity back to God.

6. **The Blood of Justification** (Rom. 5:9): This verse emphasizes that believers are justified before God by the blood of Christ. It underscores the significance of Jesus's sacrifice in securing salvation and protection from God's judgment. Justification is the act of God's grace by which He declares a person righteous and forgives their sins, considering them as if they had never sinned.

7. **The Blood of Propitiation** (Rom. 3:25): Propitiation refers to the act of appeasing or satisfying the wrath of God. In this context, the blood of propitiation is understood as the sacrificial blood of Jesus Christ shed on the cross to satisfy God's justice and reconcile humanity to

Himself. All human beings are sinners and deserve God's wrath and punishment. However, God, in His love and mercy, provided a way for reconciliation through Jesus Christ. The shedding of Jesus's blood is seen as the ultimate sacrifice, which fully satisfies God's righteous anger and wrath against sin.

8. **The Sin-Cleansing Blood** (1 John 1:7b): This verse highlights the cleansing power of Jesus's blood, emphasizing its ability to purify believers from all sin. It signifies an assurance of God's grace and forgiveness. It highlights the transformative and liberating power of Jesus's sacrifice, reminding believers that their sins are not only forgiven but completely and thoroughly cleansed – 100%. The cleansing power of the blood of Jesus is sufficient to cover sins of the past, present, and future.

9. **The Blood of Sanctification** (Heb. 9:13–14): This passage compares the temporary purification rituals of the Old Testament to the permanent and ultimate purification achieved through Christ's blood. It emphasizes the superiority and efficacy of Christ's sacrifice in purifying not just the physical body but also the conscience and enabling believers to serve God.

10. **The Blood of New Covenant** (Matt. 26:28): Jesus spoke these words during the Last Supper, indicating that his blood would be shed as part of a new covenant, which would bring forgiveness of sins. This emphasizes the sacrificial nature of Jesus's death and the essential role of his blood in obtaining forgiveness. It signifies the means by which believers are justified, and a new relationship with God is made possible. It is a central concept in Christian theology, particularly within the context of salvation and the understanding of Jesus's role as the Savior.

11. **The Innocent Blood** (Matt. 27:4): Judas Iscariot made this statement and expressed remorse for betraying Jesus, whom he considered to be innocent. While this verse does not directly address the efficacy of Christ's blood for salvation, it reminds us of the innocence and sacrificial nature of Jesus, whose blood was shed for the redemption of humanity.

12. **Church-Purchasing Blood** (Acts 20:28): This verse emphasizes the value of the church, purchased by the blood of Christ. It does not mean the visible church building but the invisible church, that is, the believers. It highlights the high price paid for the redemption and well-being of believers, emphasizing the importance of Christ's blood in securing salvation.

13. **The Blood of Eternal Redemption** (Heb. 9:12): This verse emphasizes the uniqueness and efficacy of Christ's sacrifice, contrasting it with the temporary sacrifices of the Old Testament. It emphasizes that through his own blood, Christ obtained eternal redemption, highlighting the essential role of his blood in securing salvation.

14. **The Blood of Boldness** (Heb. 10:19–20): This passage emphasizes that through the blood of Jesus, we have confidence to enter the Most Holy Place. In the Old Testament, only the high priest was allowed to enter the Most Holy Place once a year, but now, through Jesus's sacrifice, all believers have access to God's presence. The blood of Christ represents the atoning sacrifice that opens the way for us to approach God.

15. **The Blood of Full Assurance** (Heb. 10:22): Here, the writer encourages believers to approach God with sincerity and full assurance of faith. The reference to "having our hearts sprinkled" indicates the cleansing effect of the blood of Jesus. It symbolizes the forgiveness of sins and the removal of guilt and condemnation. The blood of Christ plays a crucial role in purifying our conscience and allowing us to draw near to God in worship and fellowship.

16. **The Blood of Mediator** (Heb. 12:23–24): This passage speaks of the church, specifically those who are part of the new covenant through faith in Christ. The "sprinkled blood" refers to the blood of Jesus, which has a superior message compared to the blood of Abel. Abel's blood cried out for justice and vengeance, but Jesus's blood speaks of mercy, redemption, and reconciliation. Through His blood, believers have access to God, and Jesus serves as the mediator between God and humanity.

17. **The Blood of Everlasting Covenant** (Heb. 13:20): This verse highlights the blood of the eternal covenant, which refers to Jesus's sacrificial death and resurrection. It is through His shed blood that God brought Jesus back from the dead. The blood of Christ is instrumental in the reconciliation of humanity with God, and it demonstrates God's faithfulness to His covenant promises.

18. **The Sin-Washing Blood** (Rev. 1:5): This verse affirms Jesus's redemptive work through His blood. It highlights His role as the faithful witness, the firstborn from the dead, and the ruler of kings. Jesus's love for us is demonstrated by His act of freeing us from sin through His shed blood. It is through His blood that our sins are forgiven and we are reconciled to God.

19. **The Blood of Victory over Satan** (Rev. 12:11): This highlights two key aspects. Firstly, the blood of the Lamb, symbolizing the sacrificial death of Jesus, is central to the victory of believers. It is through the redemptive. Christ's blood is able to overcome sin, evil, and the accuser. Secondly, the word of their testimony refers to the proclamation of their faith in Jesus Christ. The testimony of believers, their steadfast commitment to Christ even in the face of persecution, becomes a powerful weapon against the forces of darkness.

20. **No Substitute for Blood** (Heb. 9:22): The shedding of Jesus's blood is seen as the means by which this forgiveness and salvation are made possible. The blood of Christ is regarded as a powerful symbol of redemption, cleansing, and restoration. The significance of the blood of Christ goes beyond the physical aspect of blood itself. Rather, it represents the sacrificial death of Jesus and the complete offering of himself for the sake of humanity. It is through faith in the person and work of Jesus, including his shedding of blood, that a believer can receive salvation and eternal life.

Overall, these verses emphasize the necessity and efficacy of the blood of Christ for salvation. They highlight the sacrificial nature of Jesus's death and his ability to cleanse believers from sin, reconcile humanity to God, bring forgiveness, obtain eternal redemption, and enable believers to serve and live for God. The blood of Christ is considered central to the Christian understanding of salvation and the forgiveness of sins.

11. ETERNAL LIFE

The promise of eternal life holds great significance as it assures believers of their ultimate destiny and hope beyond the earthly realm. It provides comfort and reassurance that their relationship with God is not confined to this present life but extends into eternity. It's important to note that while eternal life is a crucial aspect of Christian salvation, it is not solely focused on the duration of life but also encompasses the quality of life in a restored and redeemed state with God. It involves knowing God, experiencing His love, and participating in His divine nature.

1. **It is found exclusively in Jesus:** (1 John 5:11–12) There are no secret doors into the commonwealth of the eternally happy! There is only one entry point and one pass code. His name is Jesus. And this is the testimony, that God gave us eternal life, and this life is in his Son.

2. **It is received by believing in Jesus:** (John 3:16). One may only enter eternal life by faith, that is, by believing in Christ, trusting in his work, and treasuring his supreme worth. And as Moses lifted up the serpent in the wilderness, so must the Son of Man be lifted up, that whoever believes in him may have eternal life. "For God so loved the world that He gave His only begotten Son, that whoever believes in Him should not perish but have everlasting life."

3. **It is the only satisfying option for the hungry and thirsty soul:** (John 4:13–15) When Jesus met the Samaritan woman at the well, she was hungry and hurting, reeling from her sin-stained past. He speaks to this woman of his ability to satisfy the quenching thirst of her soul. How does he do this? He gives eternal life.

4. **It is a gift of God's grace:** (Rom. 6:23) We do not earn this life, nor do we merit its continuation. The experience of this life is all of grace. "For the wages of sin is death, but the free gift of God is eternal life in Christ Jesus our Lord."

5. **Eternal life is knowing the Person of Jesus Christ:** (John 17:3) It is an important passage in this regard, as Jesus prays, "And this is eternal life, that they may know You, the only true God, and Jesus Christ whom You have sent." Here, Jesus equates "eternal life" with a knowledge of God and of the Son.

6. **Eternal life begins in the present, the here and now:** (John 6:47) Jesus described eternal life in the present tense. Thus, eternal life is not just in the future but is a present position of the believer, which continues into the future.

7. **We can be certain that we have now:** (1 John 5:13). John's goal was to provide clarity and confidence to those who believe in Christ. He wanted them to know that eternal life was to be enjoyed by experience as they believe. In other words, for all who presently believe in Christ, there is eternal life to be presently enjoyed!

8. **We need to receive Christ's invitation:** (Rev. 22:17b) Right now, every sinner is invited to know Christ and receive eternal life. "Come" And let him who thirsts come. Whoever desires, let him take the water of life freely."

Eternal life is not simply the quantity (how long) but also the quality of the life (how good). The happiness, satisfaction, freedom, confidence, comfort, and humility that come to the believer are the beams that radiate from the center of the gospel. This sight and warmth we feel as Christians is what I mean by quality of life. It is that colors in our concept of duration of life. It is real life indeed! And it lasts forever!

12. THE GOSPEL OF SALVATION

John 3:16: "For God so loved the world that He gave His only begotten Son, that whoever believes in Him should not perish but have everlasting life.' It encapsulates the central message of the Christian faith and beautifully portrays the relationship between God and humanity. Let's explore the verse in two parts: God's part and man's part. The term 'gospel' in Greek is 'Euaggelion', which translates to 'good news' or 'good tidings'" (Unger 1988, 493).[3]

The Assurance of Salvation

In the context of Christianity, the gospel of Jesus Christ refers to the central message of salvation through Jesus Christ's life, death, and resurrection.

1. **God's Part:** "Love and Give"
   Our God is the God of love. "For God so loved the world . . ." That is what makes it impossible for the human mind to comprehend the love of God. Love demands sacrifice. Love produces action. God has proved His love by giving His Son. To save you, He had to sacrifice His Son.)

   1) For God so loved the world: The verse begins by expressing the immense love of God for the world. God's love is not limited to a specific group or a select few; it extends to the entire world. This love is characterized by its unconditional nature, surpassing human comprehension. God's love is deep, sacrificial, and all-encompassing. Salvation starts with God. You had nothing to do with it. Before you were born, God provided it for you.

   2) He gave His only begotten Son: The love of God is not merely expressed in words or emotions; it is demonstrated through action. God's love for humanity compelled Him to give His only begotten Son, Jesus Christ. Jesus is described as the Son of God, who came into the world to reveal God's love, bring salvation, and reconcile humanity to Himself. The act of giving His Son displays the magnitude of God's love and the lengths to which He was willing to go to save humanity from the consequences of sin.

2. **Man's Part:** "Believe and Have Eternal Life"
   Perhaps you think that because God had provided salvation, there is nothing for you to do. What a mistake! Can you not see that you must accept God's offer? It is one thing for the doctor to prescribe medicine for you, but what good will it do unless you take it? You will have to receive Jesus Christ if you are ever to be saved.

   1) Whoever believes in Him should not perish: The verse emphasizes the role of faith in receiving the benefits of God's love and the sacrifice of His Son. Belief in Jesus Christ is the crucial response to God's love and the foundation of salvation. This belief involves placing one's trust and confidence in Jesus as the Savior and acknowledging Him as the Son of God. Through faith in Jesus,

individuals are saved from the eternal separation from God, often referred to as perishing.

2) But have everlasting life: The second part of man's response is the promise of eternal life. Those who believe in Jesus not only receive forgiveness of sins and deliverance from condemnation but also gain the gift of everlasting life. Everlasting life refers to a quality of life that begins in the present and continues throughout eternity in the presence of God. It is a life marked by a deep, intimate relationship with God and the hope of being with Him forever. The offended dies to set the offender free.

3. The "Greatest" from John 3:16
(1) The greatest Giver is "God." (2) The greatest gift is "His Son." (3) The greatest sacrifice is that "He gave." (4) The greatest offer is that "God so loved." (5) The greatest simplicity is to "believe." (6) The greatest receiver is "whoever believes in Him." (7) The greatest invitation is "the world." (8) The greatest promise is that we "should not perish." (9) The greatest inheritance is "everlasting life."

G-O-S-P-E-L

God so loved the world that He gave His
    Only begotten
        Son; whoever believes in Him should not
            Perish, but have
                Everlasting
                    Life.

John 3:16 reveals the incredible depth of God's love for humanity. It speaks of God's willingness to sacrifice His only Son, Jesus Christ, for the redemption and salvation of the world. Through Jesus, God offers the gift of eternal life to anyone who believes in Him. This verse encapsulates the core message of the Christian faith, emphasizing the importance of faith and God's love as the path to eternal life. It serves as a reminder of the incredible love and grace that God extends to all people, and it invites us to respond to this love by putting our faith in Jesus Christ. May this verse continue to inspire and resonate with believers, reminding us of the immeasurable love of God and the hope we have in Him.

13. PEACE

The Christian doctrine of peace is a fundamental aspect of the teachings of Jesus Christ and is central to the overall message of Christianity. It encompasses various theological, ethical, and practical dimensions that guide believers in their pursuit of inner peace, harmonious relationships, and the promotion of peace in the broader world. The doctrine of peace is deeply rooted in the Bible, particularly in the teachings of Jesus and the New Testament writings. Let's explore the key aspects of this doctrine:

Some Elements of Peace:

1) Upward Peace "Peace with God" (Rom. 5:1) The Christian doctrine of peace begins with the concept of reconciliation between humanity and God. According to Christian belief, sin creates a separation between humans and God, leading to spiritual conflict and unrest. Through the sacrificial death and resurrection of Jesus Christ, Christians believe that a way has been opened for individuals to be reconciled with God, thereby finding spiritual peace.

2) Inward Peace "Peace Within" (John 14:27) The Christian teaching on peace extends to an inner sense of tranquility and well-being. This inner peace is often described as a fruit of the Holy Spirit, as mentioned in Galatians 5:22–23. It is a result of one's faith and relationship with God, providing a sense of stability and contentment even in the midst of life's challenges.

3) Outward Peace "Peace with Others" (Matt. 5:9) Jesus emphasized the importance of peacemaking and reconciliation in his teachings. In the Sermon on the Mount. he blessed the peacemakers and taught that reconciliation with others should take precedence over hostility and conflict. The apostle Paul also emphasized the call to be ambassadors of reconciliation, urging believers to work toward restoring broken relationships (2 Cor. 5:18–20).

4) Onward Peace "Eternal Peace" (Isaiah 2:4, 11:6, 9:7) It is a vision of peace during millennium. It is believed to be a period of a thousand years of peace and righteousness under Christ's reign. During that time of peace, they shall beat their swords into plowshares and the wolf also shall dwell with the lamb. His government and its peace will never end.

Love and Forgiveness: Love and forgiveness are integral components of the Christian doctrine of peace. Jesus taught his followers to love their enemies and forgive those who wrong them (Matt. 5:43–48). This approach is rooted in the understanding that God's love and forgiveness extend to all, regardless of their faults.

Social Justice and Advocacy: The Christian doctrine of peace isn't limited to personal relationships but extends to societal issues. Many Christians are called to engage in efforts to promote justice, alleviate suffering, and work toward a more just and equitable world. This often involves advocating for the rights of the marginalized, addressing poverty, and opposing violence and oppression.

The Kingdom of God: Christians believe in the eventual establishment of the kingdom of God, a state of perfect peace and harmony. This belief shapes their view of the future and encourages them to strive for peace and justice in the present world.

Nonviolence: Many Christian traditions uphold the principle of nonviolence, inspired by Jesus's teachings and his example of enduring suffering without retaliation. This principle is often associated with figures like Mahatma Gandhi and Martin Luther King Jr., who incorporated nonviolent resistance into their quests for justice and social change.

In summary, the Christian doctrine of peace encompasses the pursuit of spiritual peace, reconciliation with God, inner tranquility, peacemaking, love, forgiveness, social justice, and nonviolence. It reflects the teachings and example of Jesus Christ, inspiring believers to foster peace within themselves, their relationships, and the world around them. Ultimately, the peace that Christ provides is rooted in the reconciling work of God through

Jesus's life, death, and resurrection. It is a gift of grace and a manifestation of God's love for humanity. By embracing this peace and allowing it to shape their lives, believers can experience a deep sense of fulfillment and find true purpose in their relationship with God and others.

14. PROPITIATION

The apostle Paul explains this in Romans 3:25a, saying, "whom God set forth as a propitiation by His blood, through faith, to demonstrate His righteousness…" The biblical propitiation for salvation refers to the sacrificial death of Jesus Christ on the cross, which satisfied God's justice, reconciled humanity to God, and provided forgiveness of sins for those who put their faith in Jesus Christ.

John Stott writes, "God does not love us because Christ died for us; Christ died for us because God loved us. If it is God's wrath which needed to be propitiated, it is God's love which did the propitiating" (Stott 2021, 203).[4]

1. **The Meaning:** "It is the act of appeasing or making well-disposed a deity, thus incurring divine favor or avoiding divine retribution. Some Bibles translate 'Propitiation' from the Greek word '*hilasterion*.' It means the lid of the ark of the covenant (Rom. 3:25)" (Unger 1988, 1044).[5] Jesus Christ is therefore 'a propitiation.' God's righteousness, which makes sin a barrier to fellowship, and God's love, which would destroy the barrier, are revealed and satisfied in one and the same means, the gift of Christ to be the Mediator between Himself and man.

2. **Right Conception of Propitiation**

    1) Atonement and Sin: In Christian theology, atonement refers to the reconciliation of humanity with God, who is considered holy and just. The concept of sin plays a central role in understanding the need for atonement. According to Christian belief, humanity is separated from God due to sin—actions or attitudes that fall short of God's perfect standard.

    2) God's Holiness and Justice: God is seen as holy and just, meaning that He is entirely pure and without sin, and His nature requires

justice to address sin's consequences. Sin disrupts the relationship between God and humanity, and justice demands that sin be dealt with accordingly.

3) Human Incapacity: In Christianity, no human can meet God's perfect standard on their own or atone for their sins. Thus, a mediator or savior is needed to bridge the gap between humanity and God.

4) Christ's Role: Jesus Christ, as the Son of God and fully divine, took on human form (incarnation) to become the perfect mediator between God and humanity. Jesus lived a sinless life and willingly sacrificed Himself on the cross.

5) Its Meaning: "Propitiation" refers to the act of appeasing or satisfying someone's wrath or anger. In this context, it implies that Jesus's sacrificial death on the cross satisfied God's justice and holiness. Through His death, Jesus took upon Himself the punishment that humanity deserved for their sins, thereby propitiating God's wrath against sin.

6) Satisfaction: The concept of satisfaction in the propitiation of Christ refers to Jesus fully fulfilling God's requirements for justice and atonement. By offering Himself as the perfect sacrifice, Jesus satisfied God's demands for justice, making it possible for humanity to be reconciled with God.

7) Redemption and Reconciliation: As a result of Christ's propitiatory sacrifice, those who believe in Him are redeemed from the power of sin and reconciled with God. This reconciliation allows believers to have a restored relationship with God, experiencing His forgiveness, love, and grace.

3. Misconceptions of Propitiations:

1) Misunderstanding God's Wrath: One misconception is that God is portrayed as a vengeful and angry deity who needed appeasement through the sacrifice of Jesus. This view can lead to a skewed understanding of God's nature and character, emphasizing wrath

over love and mercy. In Christian theology, God's justice and holiness are crucial aspects, but they are always balanced by His love and desire for reconciliation.

2) Viewing Jesus as a Payment to an Angry God: Another misconception is the idea that Jesus's sacrifice was like a payment to God to satisfy His wrath. This view may give the impression that God needed something from us (the sacrifice of Jesus) to be willing to forgive humanity, which undermines the concept of God's grace and unconditional love.

3) Separating the Trinity: Some people mistakenly see Jesus's role as separate from the Father and the Holy Spirit. In reality, the doctrine of the Trinity teaches that God is one being in three persons. The work of Jesus in propitiation is not independent of the Father's will or the Holy Spirit's work but is a unified expression of God's plan for redemption.

4) Limited Understanding of Sin: Misconceptions can arise when people underestimate the seriousness of sin and its impact on human beings. Without recognizing the depth of sin's effects, it's challenging to grasp the significance of Jesus's sacrifice to restore the broken relationship between humanity and God.

5) Seeing the Cross as the End: Some individuals may perceive Jesus's death on the cross solely as an act of atonement without fully understanding the significance of His resurrection. The resurrection is essential in Christian theology as it demonstrates victory over sin and death, providing the hope of eternal life for believers.

6) Legal Transaction Model: Some people might view the propitiation as a mere legal transaction where Jesus took the punishment on behalf of sinners, but the relationship between God and humanity is much more profound than a legal exchange. It's about restoration, reconciliation, and God's desire to bring us close to Him.

7) Ignoring God's Initiative: It is essential to emphasize that propitiation was God's initiative out of love for humanity. Jesus's sacrifice

was not a last-minute attempt to appease an angry God but a part of God's plan from the beginning to redeem and reconcile humanity to Himself.

In conclusion, the message of propitiation in Christ resounds with everlasting significance. It is the very essence of God's unconditional love and compassion for humanity, demonstrated through the selfless sacrifice of Jesus on the cross. Through Christ's propitiation, we find redemption, forgiveness, and reconciliation with God, opening the pathway to eternal life and communion with our Creator.

15. THE ATONEMENT

The doctrine of atonement in Christ is a central belief in Christian theology that seeks to explain the significance of Jesus Christ's sacrificial death and its implications for the salvation of humanity. Atonement refers to the process of reconciling or making amends for sin and estrangement between humans and God. According to Christian belief, humanity is inherently sinful and separated from God due to the disobedience of the first human beings, Adam and Eve, in the garden of Eden. This original sin has resulted in a broken relationship with God and the inability of humanity to bridge the gap on its own. Jesus Christ is the ultimate sacrifice for the redemption and forgiveness of sins. His incarnation as a fully human and fully divine being allowed him to represent God and humanity in a unique way.

1. **Double Obedience of Jesus Christ:**
    Active Obedience: If Christ had only earned forgiveness of sins for us, then we would not merit heaven. Our guilt would have been removed, but we would simply be in the position of Adam and Eve before they had done anything good or bad … For this reason, Christ had to live a life of perfect obedience to God in order to earn righteousness for us. He had to obey the law for his whole life on our behalf so that the positive merits of his perfect obedience would be counted for us.
    Passive Obedience: Christ's suffering and dying for our sin is called his "passive obedience." The penalty Christ bore in paying for our sins was suffering in both his body and soul throughout his life... In predicting the coming of the Messiah,

Isaiah said he would be "a man of sorrows and acquainted with grief" (Isai. 53:3) ... It was especially on the cross that Jesus' sufferings for us reached their climax, for it was there that before the penalty for our sin and died in our place (Grudem 2022, 305-307).[6]

2. **The Purpose of Atonement:**
The atonement of Jesus Christ is considered to be an act of divine love, mercy, and grace, providing forgiveness and reconciliation between God and humanity. The atonement is believed to have achieved several purposes.

1) It satisfied the demands of divine justice by paying the penalty for human sin, which is understood to be death. Jesus's death is seen as taking the punishment that humanity deserved upon himself, thus offering forgiveness and redemption.

2) The atonement is seen as a demonstration of God's love for humanity, as Jesus willingly gave his life to reconcile humanity with God.

3) Finally, the atonement is to have defeated the power of sin and death, offering the possibility of eternal life to those who accept Jesus's sacrifice and have faith in him. In the substitutionary atonement, Jesus is seen as a substitute for humanity, taking their place and bearing the punishment for sin, and the moral influence theory highlights the transformative power of Jesus's sacrifice in inspiring humans to live righteous lives.

3. **Old and New Testaments:**

1) In the Old Testament, the primary means of atonement was through sacrificial offerings and rituals. The Israelites believed that sin created a separation between them and God, and atonement was necessary to restore that broken relationship. The Day of Atonement, or Yom Kippur, held great significance in the Old Testament. On this day, the high priest would enter the Most Holy Place in the tabernacle or temple and make atonement for the sins

of the people through the sacrificial blood of animals. The blood of the sacrifices symbolized the covering or removal of sin, allowing the people to be reconciled with God (Lev. 16).

2) In the New Testament, the concept of atonement takes on a deeper and more profound meaning through the person and work of Jesus Christ. Jesus, as the Son of God, came to fulfill the Old Testament prophecies and provide the ultimate atonement for humanity's sins. Jesus's death on the cross serves as the perfect sacrifice for the sins of humanity. Through his sacrificial death, Jesus took upon himself the punishment that humanity deserved for their sins, offering forgiveness and reconciliation with God to all who believe in him. The New Testament describes Jesus as the "Lamb of God" (John 1:29), drawing a parallel between his sacrificial death and the animal sacrifices of the Old Testament. Jesus's sacrifice is seen as once-for-all, providing a complete and permanent atonement for the sins of humanity.

Over the centuries, different theories of atonement have been proposed, including the ransom theory, satisfaction theory, penal substitution theory, and the moral influence theory, among others. Each theory emphasizes different aspects of the atonement but ultimately seeks to explain how Jesus's death and resurrection bring about salvation for humanity. In summary, the Old Testament atonement involved sacrificial offerings and rituals as a temporary means of restoring the broken relationship between God and humanity. The New Testament atonement, fulfilled through Jesus's sacrificial death on the cross, provides a complete and permanent reconciliation with God for all who believe in him.

16. RECONCILIATION

The need for reconciliation with God arises from the concept of sin, encompassing any act contrary to God's will. Sin creates a separation between humanity and God, disrupting the relationship. Jesus's sacrificial death on the cross serves as the remedy, paying the price for human sins and providing forgiveness. By embracing faith in Jesus and accepting His sacrifice, individuals can be forgiven and restored to a right relationship with God. This reconciliation is deemed essential as it addresses the root issue of sin, offering a path to forgiveness, restoration, and eternal life in God's presence. It brings about spiritual transformation, guidance, and a renewed sense of purpose in life, as outlined in 2 Corinthians 5:18–19.

1. **Its Meaning:** Theologically, reconciliation denotes the new relationship of the depraved human being with God on the foundation of the sacrifice of Christ on the cross. The act of reconciliation calls on people to refrain from their revolt against God and turn to God with a new attitude.

2. **Its Need:** The word reconciliation means to unite two parties who are estranged. It denotes that one has given offense, and the other has taken umbrage or is displeased by it, in consequence of which there is a breach between them. Instead of friendship, there is a state of hostility existing; instead of amity there is enmity, which results in separation and alienation between them.

3. **Its Benefits:** In Colossians 1:20–23, the apostle Paul discusses the benefits and results of Jesus's reconciliation for believers. Let's explore these verses and understand their significance:

    1) Make Peace between Man and God: Colossians 1:20 states, "and by Him to reconcile all things to Himself...having made peace through the blood of His cross." This verse emphasizes that Jesus's sacrificial death on the cross has the power to reconcile all things to God. Through His blood, Jesus made peace between humanity and God, bridging the gap caused by sin.

    2) Restoration of Relationship: Colossians 1:21 says, "And you, who once were alienated an enemy in your mind by wicked words, yet now He has reconciled." Before accepting Christ, believers were separated from God, alienated, and considered enemies in their minds due to their sinful behavior. However, through Jesus's reconciliation, believers can be restored to a right relationship with God, becoming His friends and children.

    3) Presenting Holy and Blameless: Colossians 1:22 states, "in the body of His flesh through death, to present you holy, and blameless,

and above reproach in His sight." Through Jesus's sacrifice, believers are reconciled to God and presented as holy and blameless in His sight. This refers to the imputed righteousness of Christ upon believers, where their sins are forgiven, and they are regarded as righteous through faith in Jesus.

4) Firm and Secure: Colossians 1:23a says, "If indeed you continue in the faith, grounded and steadfast..." The reconciliation accomplished by Jesus provides believers with a firm and secure foundation in their faith. By continuing in faith and holding onto the hope offered through the gospel, believers can experience the steadfastness and assurance that comes from being reconciled to God.

5) Not Drifted Away: Colossians 1:23b states, "are not moved away from the hope of the gospel which you heard, which was preached to every creature..." The reconciliation brought about by Jesus safeguards believers from drifting away from the truth. By keeping the gospel at the center of their lives and embracing it fully, believers are protected from being led astray by false teachings or worldly influences.

The message of reconciliation underscores the transformative work of God in restoring the broken relationship between humanity and Himself through Christ. Reconciliation is both an accomplished fact and an ongoing mission. God, in His grace, took the initiative to reconcile the world to Himself, not counting people's sins against them but instead, offering forgiveness through the atoning sacrifice of Jesus Christ.

17. INHERITANCE

The doctrine of inheritance in Christ is a fundamental belief within Christian theology that emphasizes the spiritual blessings and privileges believers receive through faith in Jesus Christ. This concept is based on the teachings of the New Testament, particularly in the writings of the apostles Paul and Peter.

1. **Old Testament Views of Inheritance** (Num. 18:20): In the Old Testament, the concept of inheritance primarily revolved around the

allocation of land and possessions within the tribes of Israel. The passage in Numbers 18:20 states, "Then the Lord said to Aaron, 'You shall have no inheritance in their land, nor shall you have any portion among them. I am your portion and your inheritance among the children of Israel.'" This passage highlights the unique position of the Levites, who were not allocated a specific portion of land like the other tribes of Israel. Instead, God declared Himself to be their inheritance, indicating that they would be provided for by the offerings and tithes of the people.

2. **New Testament Views of Inheritance** (Rom. 8:17a): In the New Testament, the concept of inheritance takes on a more spiritual meaning, particularly in relation to believers in Jesus Christ. Romans 8:17a states, "and if children, then heirs- heirs of God and joint heirs with Christ…" This verse emphasizes the idea that believers in Christ are considered heirs of God. As children of God, they have a share in the inheritance that comes through Christ. This inheritance includes the blessings, promises, and eternal life that are granted to those who have faith in Jesus.

3. **The Major Difference of OT and NT:** The major difference between the Old Testament and New Testament views of inheritance lies in their focus and nature. In the Old Testament, inheritance primarily pertained to physical possessions, land, and provisions within the nation of Israel. It was tied to the earthly and temporal aspects of life. In contrast, the New Testament views inheritance in a more spiritual sense. It is concerned with the eternal blessings and promises that believers receive through their relationship with God and Jesus Christ. This inheritance is not limited to material possessions but encompasses salvation, forgiveness, adoption into God's family, and the promise of eternal life.

4. **The Doctrine of Inheritance in Christ**

    1) Adoption as Children of God: (Gal. 4:5) Through faith in Jesus, believers are adopted into God's family as His children. This adoption establishes an intimate and loving relationship between God and His followers, with all the rights and privileges of being part of God's household.

THE WAY OF SALVATION

2) Joint Heirs with Christ: (Rom. 8:17) As adopted children of God, believers are considered joint heirs with Jesus Christ. This means that they inherit the spiritual blessings and promises that were given to Christ, who is seen as the firstborn among many brothers and sisters.

3) Redemption and Forgiveness of Sins: (Eph. 1:7) In Christ, believers receive redemption from their sins and forgiveness through His sacrificial death on the cross. This redemption restores their relationship with God and grants them eternal life.

4) Inheritance of God's Kingdom: (1 Cor. 6:9-11) The doctrine emphasizes that believers are heirs to God's kingdom and will share in the glories and joys of the heavenly realm. This inheritance is not based on personal merit but is a gift of God's grace.

5) Sealing with the Holy Spirit: (Eph. 1:13-14) Upon believing in Christ, believers are sealed with the Holy Spirit. This seal represents the presence and guarantee of God's ownership over His people, securing their inheritance and salvation until the day of redemption.

6) Spiritual Blessings and Gifts: (1 Cor. 12, 14) In Christ, believers receive various spiritual blessings and gifts, such as wisdom, spiritual insight, and the fruits of the Holy Spirit. These gifts are given to empower them in their Christian walk and serve others within the body of Christ.

7) Eternal Inheritance: (1 Peter 1:3-5) Peter refers to this inheritance as a living hope that commences with praise to God, recognizing His immense mercy. This underscores the enduring hope bestowed upon believers through the resurrection of Jesus Christ. It is imperishable and safeguarded by the power of God.

The Christian inheritance is both a present reality and a future hope. It is a gift of grace, secured by Christ's work and preserved by God's power. The inheritance encourages us believers to live faithfully, with the assurance that their ultimate reward is kept secure in heaven, awaiting the day of full realization in God's eternal kingdom. The path to the believer's glorious inheritance involves perseverance through trials and suffering, reflecting the life of Christ.

18. PREDESTINATION

John Calvin developed a theological system that became known as Calvinism, and a key element of this system is his doctrine of predestination. Predestination is the belief that before the creation of the world, God has already determined the eternal destiny of every individual, whether they will be saved (elected) or damned "reprobated." (Eph. 1:5)

"According to the 'whosoever will' model, God loves and desires to save every person, Christ died for every person, and anyone can respond in repentance and faith to the message of the gospel and be saved" (Harwood 2022, 630).[7]

1. **Strengths and Weak Points of Predestination**

    1) Strengths:

        a. Emphasis on God's Sovereignty: Predestination highlights the absolute sovereignty of God in determining human salvation, emphasizing that salvation is solely a result of God's grace and not dependent on human actions.

        b. Assurance for the Elect: For those who believe they are part of the elect, the doctrine provides a strong sense of assurance and comfort, knowing that their salvation is secure and not subject to change.

        c. Reverence and Awe for God: The belief in predestination can lead to a profound sense of reverence and awe for God's mysterious and incomprehensible ways.

    2) Weaknesses

        a. Lack of Human Responsibility: Critics argue that predestination seems to negate human responsibility and free will.

If everything is determined by God's will, it raises questions about the accountability of human actions.

   b. Troubling Implications: The doctrine of predestination can be troubling to some individuals, as it raises questions about God's fairness and love, especially for those who are considered reprobate from the beginning without any chance of salvation.

   c. Limited Evangelism: Some critics argue that the belief in predestination might reduce the motivation for evangelism, as the belief that only the elect will be saved may lead some to believe their efforts in sharing the gospel with others are futile.

2. **Calvin's Doctrine of TULIP:** It requires a thoughtful and well-reasoned approach, as it is a complex and controversial theological concept within the framework of Calvinism. TULIP is an acronym that stands for:

   1) Total depravity: The belief that all humans are born in a state of sin and are incapable of choosing God or doing anything good without divine intervention.

   2) Unconditional election: The idea that God predestines certain individuals for salvation without considering any foreseen merit or response from them.

   3) Limited atonement: The belief that Jesus Christ's atoning sacrifice was only intended for the elect and not for all of humanity.

   4) Irresistible grace: The notion that those whom God has elected for salvation cannot resist His grace and will be drawn to faith.

   5) Perseverance of the saints: The belief that those who are truly elected by God will persevere in faith and will not lose their salvation.

3. **Our Responses to TULIP:** Many other Christians and theologians, especially from non-Calvinist traditions, raise objections to specific aspects of TULIP. Some common criticisms include:

   1) Total depravity: Critics argue that while humans may be affected by sin, they still have the capacity to choose good or reject evil through free will.

   2) Unconditional election: This aspect raises questions about the fairness and justice of God, as it seems to imply that God arbitrarily selects some for salvation while leaving others without a chance.

   3) Limited atonement: Opponents may argue that this view conflicts with the biblical message of God's love for all of humanity and the universality of Christ's sacrifice. "God desires all men to be saved" (1 Tim. 2:4a).

   4) Irresistible grace: Critics question whether God's grace truly overrides human free will, as it may suggest that God forces some to believe against their wishes.

   5) Perseverance of the saints: Some argue that the idea of "once saved, always saved" contradicts the biblical call for ongoing faith and obedience. (My opinion: Though I agree with the concept of "once saved, always saved," the eternal security of a believer stems not from their perseverance but solely from God's preservation of them)

According to Calvin's doctrine of predestination, God's decision to save or damn people is based solely on His sovereign will and not on any foreseen merit or action of the individuals themselves. In other words, God's choice is unconditional and not dependent on human efforts or choices. Those who are chosen for salvation, known as the elect, are predestined to receive God's grace and be saved, while the reprobates are destined for damnation due to their sinful nature inherited from Adam. Calvin believed that God's predestining work is secret and beyond human comprehension. It is known only to God, and humans cannot fully understand or fathom the reasons for God's choices. This doctrine places a strong emphasis on the sovereignty of God and His absolute control over human destiny.

19. UNION WITH CHRIST

The concept of Union with Christ is a central theme in Christian theology, particularly within the realm of soteriology (the study of salvation). It refers to the intimate, spiritual relationship between believers and Jesus Christ. Union with Christ encompasses various aspects and holds significant importance for understanding the Christian faith and its implications for the life of a believer.

1. **Creational Union** (2 Cor. 5:17): When a person accepts Jesus Christ as their Lord and Savior and becomes a believer, they are spiritually reborn and experience a profound change in their life. It signifies a spiritual renewal and a departure from the old sinful nature. The old way of living, characterized by sin and separation from God, is replaced by a new way of life in which the believer is reconciled to God through Jesus Christ. Being united with Christ means that believers are connected to Him in a deep and intimate relationship. They receive forgiveness for their sins, are filled with the Holy Spirit, and are empowered to live a life that is pleasing to God.

2. **Biological Union** (John 1:12): This verse speaks about receiving and believing in Jesus, which grants individuals the privilege of becoming children of God. It is not a biological union in the sense of physical or genetic connection but rather a spiritual and relational union. Union with Christ describes the intimate connection between believers and Jesus, highlighting the transformative and participatory nature of the Christian faith. The concept of union with Christ emphasizes that through faith in Jesus, believers are united with him in a profound way. This union brings about a spiritual transformation, where believers share in Christ's death and resurrection (Rom. 6:5).

3. **Organic Union** (1 Cor. 12:20): It refers to the spiritual reality that believers, through faith in Christ, are united with Him in a profound and intimate way. By stating that believers are members of Christ's body, Paul emphasizes the organic nature of this union. It is not merely a legal or positional standing but a living, vital connection. This union with Christ has profound implications for the life of a believer. Furthermore,

this organic union with Christ also has implications for the unity and interdependence of believers within the body of Christ. Overall, the concept of union with Christ as an organic union emphasizes the intimate and vital relationship between believers and Christ.

4. **Marital Union** (Eph. 5:31–32): The analogy Paul presents is that, just as a husband and wife become one flesh in marriage, so, too, do Christ and the church become united in a spiritual sense. The union between a husband and wife reflects the intimate and loving relationship that Christ has with the church. When a person puts their faith in Jesus Christ, they are spiritually united with Him. This union with Christ is seen as a profound mystery because it is a truth that is beyond human comprehension. It is not merely a legal or positional standing but a deep and intimate connection with Christ. The marital union between a husband and wife, which is a powerful and intimate bond, serves as a metaphor to help us understand the nature of our relationship with Christ.

5. **Building Union** (1 Pet. 2:5): It refers to the spiritual union that believers have with Jesus Christ through faith. When someone puts their faith in Christ, they become united with Him in a profound and mystical way. This union involves identification and participation in the life, death, and resurrection of Jesus. The imagery of believers as living stones being built into a spiritual house emphasizes the unity and corporate nature of the church. Just as individual stones come together to form a solid structure, individual believers are united with Christ and with one another to create the spiritual house of God. This spiritual house is the church, which is not a physical building but a community of believers.

In conclusion, Union with Christ emphasizes the profound spiritual connection believers have with Jesus Christ. This union is portrayed as transformative, shaping one's identity and influencing daily living. The concept underscores the Christian understanding of a deep, intimate relationship with Christ, fostering growth, redemption, and a shared purpose in the journey of faith.

20. IMPUTATION

The doctrine of imputation is closely linked to the concept of justification by faith alone. Imputed righteousness is the process whereby it attributes or credits people with the righteousness of His Son, who was the only man ever to live a perfectly sinless life. Another way to describe imputed righteousness is to say that when God looks at the one who trusts Jesus Christ for salvation, He chooses not to see that person's sin but instead sees the righteousness of Christ in that person.

"The word imputation comes from the Latin word *imputare*, meaning 'to reckon', 'to change to one's account', and relates to the problem of how sin is charged to every person" (Enns 2008, 323). [8]

There are four stages of imputations for justification

1. **The imputation of Adam's sin upon the human race** (Rom. 5:12): Adam was the first human created by God. He and his wife Eve lived in the garden of Eden, and God commanded them not to eat from the Tree of the Knowledge of Good and Evil. However, they disobeyed God's command and ate the forbidden fruit, introducing sin into the world. As a result of Adam's sin, all humanity inherited a sinful nature and became separated from God. Through Adam's sin, death entered the world, not only physical death but also spiritual death, which is separation from God. Adam acted as the representative head of the human race, and his disobedience had far-reaching consequences for all his descendants. The guilt and consequences of his disobedience are passed down to each individual; that is, the effects of that sin are transmitted to all people.

2. **The imputation of the race's sin upon Jesus Christ** (Isa. 53:6): This verse is often interpreted as a foreshadowing of Jesus Christ and his role in the redemption of humanity. Jesus, as the Son of God, came to earth as a human being, lived a sinless life, and willingly took upon himself the burden of humanity's sins. The concept of imputing human sin upon Jesus Christ is central to Christian theology and is often referred to as the doctrine of substitutionary atonement. It teaches that through

his death on the cross, Jesus took the punishment for humanity's sins, thus reconciling humans with God. This act of sacrifice is seen as an expression of God's love and mercy, providing a way for people to be forgiven and restored to a right relationship with God. Jesus, as the perfect and blameless Son of God, took upon himself the sins of humanity, bearing the consequences that we deserved.

3. **The imputation of God's righteousness upon the believer** (Rom. 4:3): Paul refers to the example of Abraham to illustrate how God's righteousness is imputed, or credited, to believers. Paul argues that Abraham's faith was counted as righteousness, not because of his works or adherence to the law, but because of his trust and belief in God's promises. Paul's main argument in Romans is that salvation comes through faith in Jesus Christ rather than through obedience to the law. He emphasizes that God's righteousness is imputed to believers when they place their faith in Jesus Christ and trust in His atoning sacrifice for the forgiveness of sins. This righteousness is not earned or achieved by human effort but is a gift from God. The imputation of God's righteousness means that, through faith in Christ, believers are declared righteous in God's sight, even though they are undeserving of such righteousness. It is a legal declaration by God, where the believer is seen as righteous because of their union with Christ and His perfect righteousness.

4. **No imputation of sin upon whom God declared righteous** (Rom. 4:8): "Blessed is the man to whom the Lord shall not impute sin." He highlights that those who have been justified by faith in Jesus Christ are in a unique position because God does not impute or count their sins against them. In the New Testament, the concept of imputation is linked to Jesus Christ's atoning sacrifice on the cross. Through faith in Jesus, believers are credited with His righteousness, and their sins are not imputed to Him. This exchange allows believers to be justified before God, with their sins forgiven and their relationship with God restored. The significance of this verse is that it emphasizes the forgiveness and grace that believers receive through faith in Christ. Instead of being burdened by sin and its consequences, believers can experience the blessedness of being declared righteous and living in a restored

relationship with God. It's important to note that this verse does not imply that believers are free to continue in sin without consequence.

Just as Adam's sin is imputed to all humanity, resulting in condemnation, Christ's perfect obedience and righteousness are imputed to believers, leading to their justification. This means that God considers the righteousness of Christ as belonging to believers, not because of their own works, but because of Christ's obedience and sacrifice. According to the idea of double imputation, on one hand, our sins are imputed to Christ, meaning He bore the penalty for our sins on the cross. On the other hand, Christ's righteousness is imputed to us, meaning that we are clothed in His righteousness. (2 Cor. 5:21, Phil. 3:9)

21. JUSTIFICATION

Simply put, to justify is to declare righteous. Justification is an act of God whereby He pronounces a sinner to be righteous because of that sinner's faith in Christ. According to Lewis and Demarest, "The doctrine of justification deals with fundamental issues of how guilty sinners are acquitted and restored to favor with a righteous God. Justification is related to other theological concepts such as forgiveness of sin, reconciliation to fellowship, the gift of eternal life, adoption into the family of God" (Lewis and Demarest 1996, 125).[9]

> **Definition:**
> "Justification may be defined as that legal act of God by which He declares the sinner righteous on the basis of the perfect righteousness of Jesus Christ. It is not an act or process of renewal, such as regeneration, conversion, and sanctification, and does not affect the condition but the state of the sinner" (Berkhof 1933, 256-257).[10]

1. **Four Kinds of Righteousness**

   1) Personal Righteousness "Condemnation" (Luke 18:9–14): This type of righteousness is exemplified by the self-righteous Pharisee in Jesus' parable. This person relies on their own moral and religious achievements, boasting about their virtues and looking down on others. However, their pride and judgmental attitude reveal a

self-centered reliance on personal works instead of acknowledging the need for God's mercy.

2) Positional Righteousness "Justification" (Luke 18:9–14): The repentant tax collector in the same parable represents this righteousness. Unlike the Pharisee, the tax collector acknowledges their sinful state and seeks God's mercy with humility. They do not rely on their own merits but recognizes their unworthiness. This type of righteousness comes from a position of humility and dependence on God's grace.

3) Practical Righteousness "Sanctification" (James 2:26): Good works are not a means to attain salvation but serve as evidence of genuine faith. James emphasizes that faith without corresponding actions is incomplete. Salvation is received through faith in Jesus Christ, and good works naturally flow from true faith, reflecting a transformed life. Practical righteousness is the demonstration of faith through good works

4) Perfect Righteousness "Glorification" (1 John 3:2): This refers to a state of complete righteousness that believers will experience in heaven. The verse from 1 John describes believers becoming like Christ when He appears. Perfect righteousness is attained only in the presence of God, either after death or at the second coming of Christ, when believers will be fully transformed into the likeness of Christ.

2. The Benefits of Justification

1) Forgiveness of Sins: Justification in Christ means that all of the believer's sins, past, present, and future, are forgiven. This forgiveness is not based on their own merits or good works but on the finished work of Christ on the cross.

2) Reconciliation with God: Through justification, believers are reconciled with God. The relationship that was broken by sin is restored, and they become children of God, able to approach Him

with confidence and enjoy a close, intimate relationship with their heavenly Father.

3) Righteousness Imputed: In justification, the righteousness of Christ is imputed to the believer. This means that believers are counted as righteous in God's sight, even though they are not inherently sinless. It is not their own righteousness but the righteousness of Christ credited to them.

4) Freedom from Condemnation: Justification ensures that believers are no longer under condemnation. They are set free from the penalty of sin, which is eternal separation from God, and they have the assurance of eternal life with Him.

5) Adoption into God's Family: Justification brings about the adoption of believers into God's family. They become heirs of God and co-heirs with Christ, sharing in the inheritance of eternal life and all the promises of God.

6) Peace with God: Through justification, believers experience peace with God. The enmity and hostility sin caused are replaced with a sense of peace and reconciliation with the Creator.

7) New Identity in Christ: Justification changes the believer's identity. They are no longer defined by their sins or shortcomings but are identified as sons and daughters of God, chosen and loved by Him.

8) Empowerment by the Holy Spirit: Upon justification, believers receive the Holy Spirit, who dwells within them. The Spirit guides, empowers, and transforms them into the likeness of Christ, enabling them to live a life that honors God.

9) Hope for the Future: Justification provides believers with hope for the future. They have the assurance that God's promises are true and that they will spend eternity with Him in heaven.

10) Access to God's Grace: Through justification, believers have access to God's grace, which sustains them in times of trial and weakness.

They can approach God with confidence, knowing that His grace is sufficient for all their needs.

3. Dangers and Warnings of Justification:

1) Legalism and Antinomianism: Misunderstanding or misapplying the doctrine of justification can lead to two extremes. Legalism refers to the belief that one can earn salvation through their good works and adherence to religious laws, minimizing the significance of faith in Christ's work. On the other hand, antinomianism is the belief that once a person is justified by faith, they are exempt from moral obligations and can live without regard to God's commandments. Both extremes neglect the balance between faith and works emphasized in Christian theology.

2) Cheap grace: The doctrine of justification can be misconstrued as a license to sin without consequences. This is often referred to as "cheap grace," where individuals believe they can receive forgiveness without genuine repentance or transformation of their lives. This misinterpretation diminishes the true cost of Christ's sacrifice and undermines the call to live a life of holiness and obedience to God.

3) Misunderstanding of faith: Some may interpret the message of justification as a purely intellectual acceptance of certain beliefs about Jesus without genuine heart transformation. True faith involves not only belief in Christ but also a surrender of one's life to Him, resulting in a changed character and a desire to follow God's will.

4) Division and controversies: Throughout Christian history, the interpretation of the doctrine of justification has been a source of division and theological debates. Different denominations and theologians have various views on the nature and extent of justification, leading to disagreements and potential schisms within the church.

5) Lack of emphasis on sanctification: While justification is essential, it is only the beginning of the Christian journey. The danger lies in focusing solely on being declared righteous without sufficient

attention to the process of sanctification, where believers are progressively transformed into the image of Christ through the work of the Holy Spirit.

6) Misleading views of God: If not properly understood, the message of justification can present a skewed view of God, making Him appear primarily concerned with punishment and judgment rather than love and mercy. This could lead to fear-based relationships with God, hindering the development of a deeper, loving, and trusting connection.

7) Downplaying the role of repentance: Justification is closely linked to repentance, which involves recognizing and turning away from sin. An incomplete understanding of justification may downplay the significance of genuine repentance, preventing individuals from fully experiencing the freedom and transformation that come through turning away from sin.

4. Compare between Paul and James

Paul	James
1. Faith	1. Works
2. Root of righteousness	2. Fruits of righteousness
3. An evangelist	3. A pastor
4. Justification	4. Sanctification
5. Grace	5. Good works
6. Salvation	6. Christian life
7. Righteous before God	7. Righteous before man
8. Intended to Self-righteous	8. Intended to Un-righteous
9. Position	9. Practice

It is essential to approach the doctrine of justification with a comprehensive understanding of its implications and its place within the broader context of Christian theology. Properly understood, the message of justification can offer great comfort, hope, and assurance to believers, leading to a life lived in gratitude and obedience to God. Overall, justification in Christ is a profound and foundational doctrine in Christianity, emphasizing the grace of God and the importance of faith in Jesus Christ for salvation and reconciliation with God. It is through this justification that Christians are made right with God and assured of their eternal destiny in His presence.

22. SANCTIFICATION

The doctrine of sanctification stands as a cornerstone of spiritual growth and transformation. Rooted in the belief in a personal relationship with God through Jesus Christ, sanctification encompasses the process by which believers are set apart and progressively transformed into the image of Christ. This journey involves the renewal of the mind, the purification of the heart, and the empowerment of the Holy Spirit to live a life of holiness and righteousness. From its biblical origins to its implications for daily living, the doctrine of sanctification shapes the Christian's pursuit of God's perfect will and exemplifies the ongoing work of divine grace in the lives of believers.

1. **Definition:** Grudem writes, "Sanctification is something that continues throughout our Christian life. The ordinary course of a Christian's life will involve continual growth in sanctification" (Grudem 2022, 399).[11]

2. **Two Steps of Sanctifications**
   Sanctification is a multifaceted concept that encompasses positional (being declared holy in Christ) and progressive (ongoing transformation into Christlikeness) aspects within Christian theology.

   1) Positional Sanctification (1 Cor. 1:30): Positional sanctification refers to the initial act of sanctification that takes place when a person believes in Jesus Christ and is justified by faith. It is also sometimes referred to as definitive sanctification. According to 1 Corinthians 1:30, this sanctification is made possible through Jesus Christ, who becomes for us wisdom from God, righteousness, sanctification, and redemption. In positional sanctification, believers are set apart and declared holy in God's sight. It is not based on their own efforts or merits but on their identification with Christ. When someone accepts Christ as their Savior, they are positionally sanctified, meaning they are considered holy and set apart for God's purposes.

2) **Practical or Progressive Sanctification (Rom. 8:9–12):** Practical or progressive sanctification is the ongoing process of being conformed to the likeness of Christ in one's daily life. It is the outworking of the positional sanctification in practical terms. Romans 8:9–12 provides insight into this process. It emphasizes the role of the Holy Spirit in the progressive sanctification of believers. In practical sanctification, believers cooperate with the Holy Spirit to grow in holiness and live in obedience to God's commands. It involves a continuous transformation of character and behavior as believers yield to the guidance and work of the Holy Spirit in their lives. It is a lifelong journey of growth and maturity in faith, marked by the pursuit of righteousness and the avoidance of sin.

In conclusion, the Christian doctrine of sanctification acts as a crucial link between Christ's redemptive work and the believer's daily spiritual journey. It entails a lifelong process of becoming more Christlike as individuals yield to the transformative power of the Holy Spirit. Sanctification is not a human achievement but a cooperative effort with God's grace, involving continual surrender, spiritual disciplines, and cultivating a heart aligned with God's desires. Through this process, believers embrace their identity as chosen by God for His purposes, empowered to illuminate the world with the truth and love of Christ. The journey of sanctification is a testimony to God's faithfulness, leading believers to a deeper understanding of His character and fostering a lasting relationship with Him.

23. JUSTIFICATION AND SANCTIFICATION

Justification and sanctification are two important theological concepts. While they are related, they have distinct meanings and purposes. In this introduction, we will compare and contrast justification and sanctification.

1. **Justification:** It is a term used to describe the act of God whereby He declares a sinner to be righteous or justified. It is a legal term that implies a courtroom setting. When a person is justified, it means that they are declared not guilty and their sins are forgiven. This act of justification is made possible through faith in Jesus Christ. According to Christian belief, Jesus's death on the cross paid the penalty for our sins,

and through faith in Him, we can receive God's forgiveness and be justified.

2. **Sanctification:** On the other hand, it refers to the ongoing process by which believers are being transformed into the image of Christ. It is a process of growth in holiness and becoming more like God. Unlike justification, which happens instantly, sanctification is a lifelong journey that involves the work of the Holy Spirit in the life of a believer. Through sanctification, believers are empowered to live a life that is pleasing to God, growing in love, righteousness, and conformity to Christ.

The Difference between Justification and Sanctification

Justification	Sanctification
1. Legal declaration	1. Continual process
2. The works of Jesus	2. The works of the Holy Spirit
3. Eternal	3. Temporal
4. External change	4. Internal change
5. Imputed righteousness	5. Imparted righteousness
6. Instantaneous	6. Progressive
7. Forensic in nature	7. Empowerment for holy living
8. God's work for a believer	8. God's work in a believer
9. Changed life	9. Changed morality
10. Positional righteousness	10. Practical righteousness
11. Declare him righteous	11. Make him righteous
12. No degree	12. Degree
13. Happens in heaven	13. Happens in him
14. Not of good works	14. Good works as evidence
15. Perfect	15. Imperfect
16. Being	16. Doing
17. Christ died for me	17. I died with Him
18. Saved from the penalty of sin	18. Saved from the power of sin
19. Saved by His death	19. Saved by His life
20. Free gift	20. Earned
21. Root	21. Fruits
22. Grace	22. Works
23. Righteous before God	23. Righteous before man
24. Eternal forgiveness	24. Temporal forgiveness
25. Un-deserved favor	25. Deserved wages
26. Salvation	26. Christian living
27. Sonship	27. Faithful servant
28. Happened in the past	28. Happens at present
29. Relationship	29. Fellowship
30. Position	30. Practice
31. Once and for all	31. Ongoing process
32. Believer	32. Achiever

33. Sinless	33. Sin less
34. State	34. Status
35. Sudden event	35. Process
36. Safe	36. Sound
37. Substitution	37. Identification
38. Taking a bath	38. Foot washing
39. Christ died for me	39. I died with Christ
40. Sin is forgiven	40. Sin is conquered
41. Boldness to enter heaven	41. Meekness to enter heaven
42. It can neither be reversed	42. It is vulnerable
43. Died once	43. Die daily
44. Car is given	44. Car is maintained
45. Works of Christ alone	45. Cooperation with the Spirit

In summary, justification and sanctification are essential aspects of the Christian faith. Justification is the act of God declaring sinners righteous through faith in Jesus Christ, while sanctification is the ongoing process of growth and transformation in holiness. Justification deals with the external status of the believer before God, while sanctification focuses on internal change and character development. Both justification and sanctification are essential for a believer's relationship with God and their journey of faith.

24. GLORIFICATION

In Christian belief, the process of glorification begins with justification, wherein a person is declared righteous before God through faith in Jesus Christ. This is followed by sanctification, which involves the ongoing process of spiritual growth and moral transformation as believers are progressively conformed to the likeness of Christ. Glorification, then, is the final step in this journey, where believers are fully and permanently transformed into the image of Christ and are brought into perfect communion with God.

1. **Some Common Elements of Glorification**

    1) Transformation of the Body: Glorification is often associated with the resurrection of the dead. According to Christian belief, at the end of time, believers who have died will be resurrected with glorified bodies. These bodies are often described as imperishable,

immortal, and incorruptible, in contrast to the mortal bodies they had during their earthly lives. This transformation is seen as a fulfillment of the promise of being united with Christ in His death and resurrection (1 Cor. 15:50–54).

2) Perfect Unity with God: Glorification is understood as the culmination of the process of sanctification, during which believers are progressively conformed to the image of Christ. In glorification, believers are believed to attain perfect unity with God, experiencing the fullness of His presence, love, and glory. This is often seen as the ultimate fulfillment of human existence and the purpose of creation (1 John 3:2).

3) Final Judgment: The concept of glorification is often closely linked to the final judgment. In various Christian traditions, it is believed that after death and resurrection, individuals will stand before God for judgment. Those who have accepted Christ's salvation and have lived according to His teachings are believed to be welcomed into God's presence and glorified, while those who have rejected God's offer of salvation may experience separation from Him (1 Cor. 3:11–15; Rev. 20:11–15)

4) Eternal State: Glorification is seen as ushering believers into the eternal state, where they will live in communion with God forever. This is often described using language of paradise, the New Jerusalem, or the new heavens and new earth, depending on the specific interpretation of eschatological passages in the Bible (1 Thess. 4:13–17).

5) Cessation of Sin and Suffering: Glorification is believed to mark the end of sin, suffering, and death for believers. In the eternal state, they will be free from the struggles and limitations of their earthly existence, experiencing complete wholeness and restoration (Rev. 21:4).

6) Worship and Praise: In the glorified state, believers are often depicted as engaging in perpetual worship and praise of God. Their

transformed hearts and minds will lead them to offer unceasing adoration to the Creator (Rev. 4:8; 7:9–12).

2. Great Privilege of a Believer:

1) Member of the Household of God (Eph. 2:19): This privilege refers to the idea that believers are part of God's family. In Christ, believers become children of God and are welcomed into a spiritual family where they have a sense of belonging and are united with other believers.

2) The Bride of Christ (John 3:29): This privilege speaks of the intimate relationship between Christ and the church. The metaphor of the bride and bridegroom is used to illustrate the deep love, commitment, and union between Christ and believers. It symbolizes the eternal bond between Christ and the church.

3) Greater than John the Baptist (Matt. 11:11): Jesus declared that among those born of women, there is none greater than John the Baptist. However, He also said that the least in the kingdom of heaven is greater than John. This privilege indicates that as believers, we have the privilege of experiencing the fullness of God's kingdom and the blessings that come with it.

4) More Blessed than OT Kings and Prophets (Luke 10:23–24): Jesus expressed that the disciples and believers of His time were privileged to see and hear what many prophets and kings longed to experience. This privilege recognizes that believers have the opportunity to witness and understand the revelation of God's truth and salvation in Jesus Christ, which the Old Testament figures eagerly awaited.

5) The Ambassador of Christ (2 Cor. 5:20): Believers are called to be ambassadors of Christ, representing Him and His message to the world. This privilege entails the responsibility and honor of sharing the good news of salvation, showing His love, and inviting others into a relationship with Him.

6) Judge of the World and Angels (1 Cor. 6:2–3): This privilege suggests that believers will have a role in judging the world and even angels in the future. It speaks of the authority and responsibility entrusted to believers by God to participate in His divine justice and judgment.

7) Kings and Priests with Christ (Rev. 1:6): In the opening chapter of Revelation, John addresses the seven churches and conveys a message from Jesus. In verse 6, it is mentioned that Jesus has made believers to be kings and priests to serve God and reign with Him. This emphasizes the royal and priestly role that believers have in Christ's kingdom.

In conclusion, glorification represents the final stage of redemption, where believers are fully transformed and perfected in the presence of God. It marks the culmination of salvation, where all races of sin are removed, and individuals are restored to their intended state of righteousness and eternal glory. The ultimate fulfillment of divine promise highlights the completion of the journey toward spiritual renewal and everlasting life in God's presence.

25. THE LAST THINGS

The Christian doctrine of "The Last Things," also known as eschatology, explores the teachings and beliefs surrounding the ultimate fate of humanity, the world, and the cosmos as understood within the context of Christianity. This doctrine delves into themes of resurrection, judgment, heaven, hell, the second coming of Christ, and the establishment of God's eternal kingdom. The Last Things hold a significant place in Christian theology, as they offer believers a perspective on the culmination of history and the ultimate fulfillment of God's plan.

1. **The Second Coming of Jesus Christ:** The second coming of Jesus Christ is described in various parts of the New Testament, including in the book of Revelation, Matthew 24, and other passages. It is believed that Jesus will return to earth in the future to judge the living and the dead and establish His eternal kingdom.

1) The Rapture: The idea of the rapture suggests that believers in Christ will be taken up to meet Him in the air before a period of tribulation on earth. 1 Corinthians 15:50–54 discusses the transformation of believers' bodies at the last trumpet, when the perishable will put on the imperishable and the mortal will put on immortality. Revelation 1:7 speaks of Jesus coming with the clouds and every eye seeing Him, including those who pierced Him. (Knight 1998, 266-267)[12]

2) The Revelation: The second stage is often referred to as the Revelation, which involves the return of Jesus Christ in power and glory. This event is described in detail in the book of Revelation, particularly in Revelation 19:11–21. According to this account, Jesus will come riding on a white horse, leading the armies of heaven, and will defeat the forces of evil in a final battle. During the Revelation, Jesus will establish His kingdom on earth, known as the millennial kingdom, which will last for a thousand years. This period is associated with peace and the fulfillment of God's promises.

2. **Two Resurrections** (John 5:27–28): "and has given Him authority to execute judgement also, because He is the Son of Man. Do not marvel at this; for the hour is coming in which all who are in the graves will hear His voice" This passage is often interpreted to refer to two distinct events of resurrection:

   1) Resurrection of Justification (the Saved): This refers to the resurrection of those who have accepted Jesus Christ as their Lord and Savior and have lived according to their faith. They are to be raised to eternal life and rewarded for their righteous deeds.

   2) Resurrection of Condemnation (the Lost): This refers to the resurrection of those who have rejected Christ and lived in disobedience or unbelief. They are to be raised for judgment and face eternal separation from God.

3. **The Great Tribulation** (Matt. 24:21): The great tribulation refers to a period of intense suffering and distress that Jesus prophesied about during his discourse on the Mount of Olives. Here's the passage in

question: "For then there will be great tribulation, such as has not been since the beginning of the world until this time, no, nor ever shall be." (Matt. 24:21). The purpose of the great tribulation is to purify and refine the faithful, testing their faith and separating true believers from those who have turned away from God. It is considered a time of judgment and a prelude to the establishment of Christ's kingdom on earth.

4. **The Millennium Reign of Jesus Christ** (Rev. 20:4–6): There are several different views on the nature and timing of the millennium. The three main perspectives are:

    1) Premillennialism: This view holds that Christ's return will occur before the millennium. According to premillennialists, Christ will establish a literal thousand-year reign on earth, where he will rule with believers who have been resurrected. This view often includes the belief in a rapture, where believers are taken up to be with Christ before a period of tribulation on earth. (Bird 2020, 339)[13]

    2) Postmillennialism: They suggest that the millennium will be brought about through the spread of the gospel and the influence of Christianity in the world. This view holds that the world will gradually be transformed and improved, resulting in a thousand-year period of peace and righteousness. After this period, Christ will return to judge the living and the dead. (Bird 2020, 333)[14]

    3) Amillennialism: It does not interpret the thousand years of the millennium as a literal period of time. Instead, it views the millennium symbolically, representing the present age of the church. They believe that Christ is currently reigning spiritually in the hearts of believers, and the binding of Satan described in Revelation 20 represents the limitations on his power to deceive the nations. According to this view, the end of the millennium corresponds to Christ's second coming and the final judgment. (Bird 2020, 336)[15]

5. **Three Thrones of Jesus Christ**

    1) The Judgment Seat of Christ (2 Cor. 5:10): It states, "For we must all appear before the judgment seat of Christ, so that each

one may receive done in the body, according to what he has done, whether good or bad" The judgment seat of Christ is the place where believers will be judged for their actions and deeds in their earthly lives. It is not a judgment of salvation but rather a judgment of rewards or loss of rewards for believers. (Thang 2022, 27)[16]

2) **The Throne of Glory** (Matt. 25:31–46): It is commonly known as the parable of the sheep and the goats. In this passage, Jesus describes the Son of Man (referring to himself) sitting on his glorious throne and separating the righteous from the unrighteous. The righteous are blessed and welcomed into the kingdom of heaven, while the unrighteous are condemned. (Thang 2022, 28)[17]

3) **The Great White Throne Judgment** (Rev. 20:11–15): It depicts a scene where the dead, small and great, stand before the great white throne, and books are opened. This judgment is for those who did not have a personal relationship with Christ and did not receive salvation during their earthly lives. It is a judgment of condemnation, where each person is judged according to their deeds and cast into the lake of fire. (Thang 2022, 28)[18]

6. **New Heaven and New Earth** (Revelation 21:1): In the Bible describes a profound and hopeful vision of the future, proclaiming, "Now I saw a new heaven and a new earth, for the first heaven and the first earth had passed away. Also there was no more sea." The imagery of a new heaven and new earth signifies a divine transformation, a culmination of God's redemptive plan. It symbolizes a future reality where God's ultimate purpose for creation is fulfilled, free from sin and corruption. This verse resonates with themes of renewal, restoration, and the establishment of God's eternal kingdom, offering believers a powerful vision of hope and the promise of a glorious future.

7. **Hell – Lake of Fire** (Rev. 20:15): Hell is mentioned as a place of eternal punishment. The verse states, "And anyone not found written in the Book of Life was cast into the lake of fire." This depiction implies that those whose names are not recorded in the Book of Life will face everlasting condemnation. Throughout the Bible, hell is described as a place of torment and separation from God. It is depicted as a fiery lake or

furnace, where the unrighteous will suffer eternal punishment for their sins. While Revelation provides symbolic and metaphorical descriptions, the concept of hell signifies a state of everlasting separation from God's presence and the experience of intense suffering.

8. **The Rewards and Crowns:** These crowns serve as metaphors for the rewards and blessings that await believers in their eternal life with God. They represent different aspects of faithful Christian living and are meant to encourage and motivate believers in their journey of faith.

   1) The Imperishable Crown (1 Cor. 9:25): This crown refers to the reward for those who exercise self-control and discipline in their spiritual lives. It is described as imperishable because it lasts for eternity.

   2) The Crown of Rejoicing (1 Thess. 2:19): Also known as the Crown of Exultation or the Crown of Joy, it represents the reward for those who have been faithful in sharing the gospel and leading others to Christ.

   3) The Crown of Righteousness (2 Tim. 4:8): This crown is promised to those who have lived a righteous and faithful life, eagerly awaiting the return of Jesus Christ. It signifies the reward of righteousness and faithfulness.

   4) The Crown of Life (Rev. 2:10): This crown is promised to those who endure trials and remain faithful to God even in the face of persecution and death. It represents eternal life and victory over death.

   5) The Crown of Glory (1 Pet. 5:4): This crown is specifically mentioned in relation to leaders or shepherds in the church. It is a reward for those who faithfully shepherd God's flock and serve as examples to others.

   6) The Crown of Gold (Rev. 4:4): This crown is seen in the heavenly scene described in Revelation, where twenty-four elders are seen wearing crowns of gold. It symbolizes honor, glory, and authority.

The Assurance of Salvation

In summary, the Christian doctrine of "The Last Things" provides a profound framework for understanding the final destiny of humanity and the cosmos. It underscores the transient nature of earthly existence and emphasizes the significance of living according to Christian values. The hope of resurrection, the assurance of divine justice, and the prospect of eternal communion with God inspire believers to pursue spiritual growth and righteousness. Overall, this doctrine encourages Christians to look beyond current challenges, focusing on the ultimate hope of a redeemed and perfected world in the presence of God.

26. THE LIFE OF JESUS CHRIST

The life of Jesus Christ is indeed qualified and vital for the salvation of humankind. As the Son of God, Jesus came to Earth in human form to offer redemption and reconcile humanity with God. His life, teachings, miracles, and sacrificial death on the cross are central to the Christian faith, demonstrating God's love and grace. Jesus emphasized love, forgiveness, and righteousness, challenging traditional practices and calling for a personal relationship with God based on faith and spiritual transformation. Through faith in Jesus, believers can have a restored relationship with God and the hope of eternal life.

1. **His Divinity:** (John 1:1–3): Christians believe that Jesus is the Son of God and that through his life, death, and resurrection, he provided salvation and redemption for humanity. Jesus is divine, part of the Holy Trinity, which consists of God the Father, God the Son (Jesus), and God the Holy Spirit. This belief is based on various scriptural passages in the Bible, such as John 1:1, which states, "In the beginning was the Word, and the Word was with God, and the Word was God." Christians interpret this verse and others as evidence of Jesus's divinity. The idea of Jesus as the Savior of the world stems from the belief that humanity is inherently sinful and separated from God. Through his death on the cross, Jesus paid the price for humanity's sins, providing a way for people to be reconciled with God. This act of sacrifice and redemption is seen as an expression of God's love and mercy toward humanity.

2. **The Seed of the Woman** (Gen. 3:15): Jesus, the Son of God, came into the world to save humanity from sin and reconcile them with God. The

reference mentioned, Genesis 3:15, is often seen as a prophetic verse that foreshadows the coming of Jesus. In that verse, God speaks to the serpent after Adam and Eve had eaten the forbidden fruit. God says, "And I will put enmity between you and the woman, and between your seed and her Seed; He shall bruise your head, and you shall bruise His heel." (Gen. 3:15). This verse is commonly interpreted as the first announcement of the Messiah, who would be born of a woman and eventually defeat the power of evil. We see Jesus Christ as the fulfillment of this prophecy, as he was born of the Virgin Mary, a descendant of Eve, and through his sacrificial death and resurrection, he overcame sin and death, qualified for the Savior.

3. **His Humanity** (John 1:14): Christians hold that Jesus, through his incarnation as a human being, fulfilled the role of the Messiah and provided salvation for humanity. Jesus is fully divine and fully human. The concept of the incarnation refers to the belief that God took on human form in the person of Jesus Christ. This is expressed in the Gospel of John, specifically John 1:14, which states, "And the Word became flesh and dwelt among us..." The significance of Jesus's humanity lies in the fact that he lived a sinless life, thereby serving as the perfect sacrifice for the forgiveness of sins. The shedding of Jesus's blood on the cross represents the atonement for humanity's sins. Without the shedding of blood, there can be no forgiveness of sins, as stated in Hebrews 9:22. The combination of Jesus's humanity and divinity is considered crucial in the Christian understanding of salvation. His humanity allows him to identify with human suffering and experience temptation, while his divinity enables him to bridge the gap between God and humanity, offering redemption and forgiveness.

4. **His Sinlessness** (2 Cor. 5:21): Jesus Christ is the only Savior due to His sinlessness. The apostle Paul writes, "For He made Him who knew no sin to be sin for us, that we might become the righteousness of God in Him." Jesus is the Son of God and the Messiah, sent by God to save humanity from sin and reconcile them with God. The belief in Jesus's sinlessness is derived from the understanding that Jesus lived a perfect and blameless life, free from any wrongdoing or moral imperfection. This sinlessness is seen as a crucial aspect of His role as the Savior, as only a sinless sacrifice could atone for the sins of humanity.

All humans are born with a sinful nature and are separated from God because of their sins. However, through faith in Jesus Christ and His sacrificial death on the cross, believers can be forgiven of their sins and restored in their relationship with God. Jesus's sinlessness is seen as an essential qualification for Him to serve as the perfect mediator between humanity and God, offering salvation to all who trust in Him.

5. **His Humility** (Phil. 2:5–11): It speaks about the humility of Jesus Christ. It highlights the selfless and humble nature of Jesus and emphasizes his role as the Savior of the world. In this passage, the apostle Paul encourages the believers in Philippi to have the same mindset as Christ, who, despite being divine, chose to humble himself and take on the form of a servant. Paul describes how Jesus willingly emptied himself of his divine privileges and became human, even going so far as to submit himself to death on the cross. The passage states that because of Jesus's humility and obedience to God's plan, God exalted him and gave him the name that is above every name. It affirms that every knee shall bow and every tongue confess that Jesus Christ is Lord, to the glory of God the Father. The humility of Jesus Christ is seen as a central aspect of his redemptive work. Through his humility, he provided an example for believers to follow, demonstrating selflessness, servanthood, and sacrificial love. His ultimate act of humility in offering himself as a sacrifice for the sins of humanity is seen as the means through which salvation and reconciliation with God are made possible.

6. **His Law-Keeping** (Matt. 5:17; Gal. 3:13): The statement reflects Jesus Christ is the only Savior because he perfectly fulfilled God's laws. Let's examine the passages to understand their context and implications. Matthew 5:17 states that Jesus is emphasizing that he did not come to abolish the law but to fulfill it. This means that Jesus, through his life, teachings, and ultimate sacrifice, fulfilled the requirements of the law, which humanity was unable to do. He demonstrated perfect obedience to God's laws, serving as a representative for humanity. Galatians 3:13 highlights the redemptive aspect of Jesus's sacrifice. Through his death on the cross, Jesus took upon himself the curse that the law pronounced upon all who failed to perfectly keep it. In doing so, he provided a means of redemption for humanity, freeing them from the condemnation brought about by their inability to keep the law perfectly. Based on

these passages, Jesus Christ is the only Savior because he fulfilled the law on behalf of humanity, offering salvation and redemption to those who place their faith in him.

7. **His Resurrection** (John 11:25): In John 11:25, Jesus says, "I am the resurrection and the life. He who believes in Me, though he may die, he shall live." These verses emphasize Jesus's role as the source of eternal life and the power of faith in Him. According to Christian doctrine, Jesus's resurrection from the dead is seen as a pivotal event in human history. It signifies His victory over sin and death and demonstrates His divine nature and authority. Through His resurrection, Jesus conquered death and opened the way for humanity to have forgiveness of sins and eternal life with God. The belief in Jesus as the only Savior is rooted in the Christian understanding that salvation comes exclusively through Him. Christians believe that Jesus, as the Son of God, willingly sacrificed Himself on the cross as an atonement for humanity's sins. The resurrection of Jesus serves as a validation and affirmation of His claims to be the Son of God and the Savior of humanity.

8. **His Ascension** (John 16:7–8): In John 16:7–8, Jesus is speaking to his disciples, explaining that it is necessary for him to depart so that the Advocate (often interpreted as the Holy Spirit) can come. The Holy Spirit's role includes convicting the world of sin, righteousness, and judgment. This passage emphasizes the importance of Jesus's departure and the subsequent coming of the Holy Spirit to continue the work of salvation and guidance. Acts 1:9 describes the moment of Jesus's ascension, where he was taken up into heaven in the presence of his disciples. The ascension signifies the completion of Jesus's earthly ministry and his return to the heavenly realm. It is affirming Jesus's divine nature and authority. While these verses highlight key moments in Jesus's life, it is important to note that the belief in Jesus as the only Savior extends beyond these specific passages. Jesus's sacrificial death on the cross and subsequent resurrection are the central events that provide salvation for all who believe in him.

9. **His Intercession** (Rom. 8:34): Christians believe that Jesus, as the Son of God, came to earth to offer salvation and reconcile humanity with God through his life, death, and resurrection. Romans 8:34 is often

cited as support for this belief. Romans 8:34 states, "Who is he who condemns? It is Christ who died, and furthermore is also risen, who is even at the right hand of God, who also makes intercession for us." This verse emphasizes that Jesus, having died and been raised to life, now sits at the right hand of God and intercedes for believers. In other words, Jesus acts as a mediator between God and humanity, advocating for those who have put their faith in him. The concept of Jesus's intercession from heaven is a fundamental aspect of Christianity that through his sacrifice and intercession, Jesus offers forgiveness of sins and eternal life to all who trust in him.

10. **His Second Coming** (John 14:2–4; Rev. 1:7a): Jesus is the Son of God who came to earth, lived a sinless life, died on the cross for the sins of humanity, and was resurrected, offering salvation and eternal life to all who believe in Him. Christians often interpret John 14:2–4 and Revelation 1:7 in relation to the second coming of Jesus Christ. In John 14:2–4, Jesus speaks to His disciples, saying, "In my Father's house are many mansions... And if I go and prepare a place for you, I will come again and receive you to Myself..." Revelation 1:7a states, "Behold, He is coming with clouds, and every eye will see Him, even they who pierced Him." These verses are often understood as referring to the future return of Jesus Christ, commonly known as the second coming. We believe that Jesus will return in glory at the end of time to judge the living and the dead and to establish His eternal kingdom.

In conclusion, the perfect and holy life of Jesus Christ is the cornerstone for our salvation. His life marked by sinless obedience to the will of God, fulfill the righteous requirement of the law on behalf of humanity. Jesus lived a life that no other human could – completely free from sin – thereby becoming the perfect sacrifice for our sins.

27. WONDERFUL EXCHANGE

The exchange position between Christ and a believer is a central concept in Christian theology. It highlights the transformative nature of faith in Jesus Christ, where believers are united with Him, exchanging their sinful nature for His righteousness. This union brings forgiveness, new life, and an ongoing process of transformation as believers seek to live in alignment with Christ's teachings and reflect His character.

1. **Born of God** (Gal. 4:4–5 NIV): It is based on the belief that Jesus, the Son of God, came down from heaven to earth, taking on human form and being born as a baby. It states: "But when the set time had fully come, God sent his Son, born of a woman, born under the law, to redeem those under the law, that we might receive adoption to sonship." This verse is often understood to emphasize that Jesus, though divine, willingly subjected himself to the limitations and conditions of humanity by being born on earth and living under the Mosaic law.

    The idea of being "born again" or "born from above" refers to the spiritual transformation or rebirth that individuals experience when they put their faith in Jesus Christ. (John 3:3-5) This transformation is possible because of Jesus's sacrificial death and resurrection, which opens the way for reconciliation with God and the gift of eternal life. In summary, the exchange of position highlights that Jesus, as the Son of God, came down from heaven to earth, taking on human form so that humanity could be redeemed and receive spiritual rebirth through faith in him.

2. **The Wrath of God** (Isa. 53:10 NIV): Isaiah 53:10 speaks about the suffering and sacrifice of the Messiah, who is Jesus Christ. The verse states, "Yet it was the Lord's will to crush him and cause him to suffer, and though the Lord makes his life an offering for sin, he will see his offspring and prolong his days, and the will of the Lord will prosper in his hand." This verse describes the Messiah's suffering and the fact that God's will is to crush him and cause him to suffer. It is believed that Jesus, through his crucifixion and death, fulfilled this prophecy by becoming the ultimate sacrifice for the sins of humanity.

    (Ephesians 2:3 NIV) describes the spiritual condition of humanity before accepting Jesus Christ. The verse says, "All of us also lived among them at one time, gratifying the cravings of our flesh and following its desires and thoughts. Like the rest, we were by nature deserving of wrath." Here, Paul is emphasizing that all people, by nature, are deserving of God's wrath because of their sinful nature and actions. In this exchange, Jesus, the sinless one, bore the punishment on behalf of sinners. He took their place and paid the price for their sins through his suffering and death on the cross.

3. **The Righteousness of God** (2 Cor. 5:21 ESV): In 2 Corinthians 5:21, the apostle Paul writes, "For our sake he made him to be sin who knew no sin, so that in him we might become the righteousness of God". This verse highlights an important theological concept known as the "great exchange" or the "double imputation." The verse expresses the idea that through Jesus Christ, an exchange takes place between believers and God. It states that God made Jesus, who was sinless, to be sin on behalf of humanity. This refers to Jesus taking upon himself the burden and consequences of sin, even though he was without sin.

In this exchange, believers, through faith in Christ, receive the righteousness of God. It means that when we put our faith in Jesus, our sins are imputed to him, and his righteousness is imputed to us. Our sins are transferred to Jesus, who paid the penalty for our sins through his death on the cross, and his perfect righteousness is credited to us. This concept is foundational to Christian theology and speaks to the idea of salvation and the atonement accomplished by Jesus. Through this exchange, believers are reconciled to God, and their sins are forgiven. They are declared righteous in God's sight, not based on their own merit or works but through the righteousness of Christ that is attributed to them.

4. **The Eternal Life of God** (John 3:16): It states: "For God so loved the world that he gave his one and only Son, that whoever believes in him should not perish but have everlasting life." This verse is often understood to highlight the exchange of positions between a dead sinner and the living Christ in terms of life and death. In this interpretation, it is believed that all human beings are sinners and separated from God, which leads to spiritual death. However, God's love for humanity is demonstrated through the sacrifice of Jesus Christ, His Son. By believing in Christ and accepting Him as their Savior, individuals can experience a spiritual transformation.

According to this understanding, through faith in Christ, believers receive forgiveness for their sins and are granted eternal life. In this exchange, the punishment for sin that leads to death is taken upon Christ, who died on the cross, while believers are offered the gift of eternal life through their relationship with Him. The interpretation provided here represents a general understanding of John 3:16 and the exchange of positions between sinners and Christ in terms of life and death.

5. **The Blessing of God** (Deut. 30:19; Gal. 3:13): In Deuteronomy 30:19, Moses is addressing the Israelites and presenting them with a choice between life and death and blessing and cursing. God is calling upon the people to make the right decisions and choose the path that leads to life and blessing, not death and cursing. The implication is that obedience to God's commands and living in accordance with His laws will result in blessings, while disobedience will bring about curses.

   Galatians 3:13 says, "Christ has redeemed us from the curse of the law, having become a curse for us (for it is written, 'Cursed is everyone who hangs on a tree')." In this verse, the apostle Paul is explaining the redemptive work of Jesus Christ. He emphasizes that Jesus became a curse for us, taking upon Himself the curse that was associated with the law. The phrase "Cursed is everyone who hangs on a tree" refers to the method of execution during that time, particularly crucifixion. Jesus, by willingly undergoing crucifixion, took upon Himself the curse that was due to sinners under the law. Through faith in Him, believers can experience a transformative exchange where Jesus takes their curse upon Himself, offering them forgiveness, reconciliation with God, and the promise of eternal life.

6. **Son of Man** (Luke 19:10; John 1:12): In Luke 19:10, Jesus states his mission: "For the Son of Man has come to seek and to save that which was lost." By referring to himself as the Son of Man, Jesus is emphasizing his role as a representative of humanity. In John 1:12, it says, "But as many as received Him, to them He gave the right to become children of God, to those who believe in His name." This verse highlights that those who receive and believe in Jesus have the privilege of becoming children of God. It signifies a change in our status and relationship with

God, where we are no longer separated from Him but are now part of His family.

The exchange of position can be understood in the context of Jesus's incarnation and sacrificial death on the cross. Jesus, who is fully divine, took on human form (the Son of Man) to identify with humanity, experience our struggles, and ultimately provide salvation for all who believe in Him. Through His sacrifice, Jesus made it possible for us to be reconciled to God and be adopted as His children. This concept of exchanging positions is rooted in the theological understanding of Jesus as the mediator between God and humanity. He bridges the gap between the divine and the human, allowing us to have a restored relationship with God and receive the blessings and privileges of being His children.

7. **Forsaken of God** (Matt. 27:46b; Heb. 13:5b): Matthew 27:46b says, "'My God, my God, why have you forsaken me?'" One interpretation suggests that when Jesus cried out these words, he was expressing his anguish and the weight of taking upon himself the sins of humanity. According to this interpretation, in that moment, Jesus experienced a temporary separation from God the Father, bearing the full weight of the world's sins. This interpretation emphasizes the sacrificial nature of Jesus's death and the depth of his identification with humanity.

   Hebrews 13:5b says, "For He Himself has said, 'I will never leave you nor forsake you.'" This verse is an assurance that God will always be with his people and will never abandon them. It emphasizes God's faithfulness and commitment to those who have a relationship with him. The theological understanding, Christ was forsaken so that we will not be forsaken, draws from the idea that Jesus, through his sacrificial death on the cross, took upon himself the forsakenness and separation from God that humanity deserved because of sin. By doing so, he made it possible for people to be reconciled with God and experience his presence and eternal relationship.

The wonderful exchange between sinless Christ and sinful humanity captures the essence of salvation. Christ, free from sin, takes on the sins of humanity, offering redemption and reconciliation. This profound exchange exemplifies divine grace, demonstrating God's love and mercy, ultimately providing a pathway for believers to experience forgiveness and restoration.

28. HOW TO PROVE FOR YOUR SALVATION

The Bible provides essential insights into the assurance of salvation. Numerous passages affirm that salvation is a result of faith in Christ and not by our own works. The Scriptures emphasize the role of God's grace in initiating and sustaining this relationship, ensuring that believers can be confident in their salvation.

1. **The conviction of sin:** (John 16:8): "He will convict the world of sin." As Christians grow in their faith, the Holy Spirit continues to convict them of areas where they need to repent and seek God's forgiveness. This is the evidence of the reality of being born again in Christ.

2. **Know that you have eternal life:** (1 John 5:13 NIV): "I write these things to you who believe in the name of the Son of God, that you may know that you have eternal life." This verse suggests that those who have faith in Jesus Christ can have assurance of eternal life.

3. **Assure your sin forgiven:** (Eph. 1:7): It says, "In Him we have redemption through His blood, the forgiveness of our sins, according to the riches of His grace." This verse emphasizes that through the sacrifice of Jesus Christ, believers can have assurance of forgiveness for their sins.

4. **A transformed life:** (2 Cor. 5:17): It states, "Therefore, if anyone is in Christ, he is a new creation; old things have passed away; behold, all things have become new." This verse highlights the transformative power of faith in Christ, suggesting that believers experience a change in their lives.

5. **More love to Christ:** (John 21:15–17): It is a conversation between Jesus and Peter after his resurrection. Jesus asks Peter three times if he loves Him, and Peter affirms his love. This passage emphasizes the importance of love and commitment to Christ.

The Assurance of Salvation

6. **Love other Christians:** (1 John 3:14–16): It speaks about love for fellow believers. It states, "We know that we have passed from death to life, because we love the brethren. He who does not love his brother abides in death." This verse emphasizes the importance of love for other Christians as a sign of being alive in Christ.

7. **Passion for souls:** (Rom. 10:1): It expresses the apostle Paul's deep concern and love for his fellow Jews who have not yet believed in Jesus. It highlights the importance of a compassionate and evangelistic attitude toward those who are lost.

8. **Loving even your enemies:** (Matt. 5:44): This teaching from Jesus encourages believers to love their enemies and pray for those who persecute them. It reflects the transformative power of love and forgiveness that can be found in a relationship with God.

9. **Hunger for the word:** (1 Pet. 2:2): This verse emphasizes the importance of desiring the pure spiritual milk of God's Word, indicating a hunger for spiritual growth and nourishment through the Scriptures.

10. **Understanding the Word:** (1 Cor. 2:12): This verse highlights the role of the Holy Spirit in helping believers understand the things freely given to them by God, including the wisdom and truths found in the Bible.

11. **Spirit-led life:** (Rom. 8:14): Being led by the Spirit means allowing the Holy Spirit to guide and direct one's thoughts, actions, and decisions. It indicates a close relationship with God and a willingness to follow His leading.

12. **Willingness to pray:** (Rom. 8:15): The verse states that believers have received the Spirit of adoption, enabling them to cry out "Abba, Father," expressing an intimate relationship with God and a willingness to communicate with Him through prayer.

13. **The discipline of God:** (Heb. 12:5–8): This passage speaks about God's discipline of His children as a sign of His love. It suggests that

if someone experiences discipline from God, it may indicate that they are His children and that He desires their growth and maturity.

14. **A joyful life:** (Phil. 4:4): This verse encourages believers to rejoice in the Lord always. It suggests that a deep and abiding joy can be found in a relationship with God, regardless of external circumstances.

15. **A peaceful life:** (Phil. 4:7): This verse speaks about the peace of God that surpasses all understanding, which guards the hearts and minds of believers. It indicates that a relationship with God can bring inner peace and tranquility, even in the midst of life's challenges. These points can be seen as characteristics or outcomes of a person's relationship with God, which may indicate their salvation.

Knowing and proving that we have been saved in Christ is a foundational aspect of the Christian experience. It is a matter of personal conviction and theological understanding. By examining the biblical foundations of salvation, witnessing the transformative work of the Holy Spirit, and experiencing the assurance provided through God's promises, believers can confidently affirm their relationship with Christ. The journey of faith involves continuous growth, assurance, and an unwavering trust in the redemptive power of Jesus Christ.

29. ETERNAL SECURITY

The believer's stand in Christ as a result of salvation is considered secure and steadfast according to Christian theology. Salvation is often understood as a transformative process where an individual accepts Jesus Christ as their Lord and Savior, acknowledging their need for redemption and forgiveness of sins. This act of faith is believed to result in a personal relationship with God and the assurance of eternal life. Christian teachings emphasize that salvation is not based on one's own efforts or merits but is a gift of God's grace. It is seen as a permanent and unchangeable state, rooted in the work of Christ on the cross. Ultimately, the security of the believer's stand in Christ find comfort and assurance in their relationship with Christ, trusting in His promises and relying on His grace to sustain them throughout their spiritual journey.

The Assurance of Salvation

Day explains that "the eternal security of the believer is this: once a sinner has been regenerated by the Word and Spirit of God, once he has received a new life and new nature and has been justified from every charge, it is absolutely impossible for him to be lost" (Day 1953, 39).[19]

1. **Salvation is secure because it is eternal life** (John 3:16): John 3:16 states, "For God so loved the world, that He gave His only begotten Son, that whoever believes in Him should not perish but have everlasting life." This verse highlights the Christian belief that through faith in Jesus Christ, believers receive the gift of eternal life. The concept of salvation and eternal life is central to Christian theology. Christians believe that salvation is a free gift of God's grace, made possible through the sacrificial death and resurrection of Jesus Christ. By accepting Jesus as their Lord and Savior and putting their faith in Him, Christians believe they are reconciled with God and have the assurance of eternal life. The belief in eternal life means that those who have placed their faith in Jesus Christ will experience an everlasting existence in God's presence. It is not contingent on one's own merits or good works but is based on God's love, mercy, and forgiveness.

2. **Salvation is secure because it is a free grace in Christ** (Rom. 3:24): The belief is that salvation is secured through the free grace of God, made possible by the sacrificial death and resurrection of Jesus Christ. In Romans 3:24, the apostle Paul writes, "being justified freely by His grace through the redemption that is in Christ Jesus" Since humanity is separated from God due to sin, and salvation is the reconciliation between God and humanity, it is believed that no one can earn salvation through their own efforts or good works because all have sinned and fall short of God's perfect standard (Rom. 3:23). Instead, salvation is a gift from God, given by His grace and received through faith in Jesus Christ. This means that salvation is not earned or merited by our actions, but it is freely given to those who trust in Christ. This understanding of salvation through grace is a central tenet of Christians and is often referred to as "sola gratia," which means "by grace alone."

3. **Salvation is secure because of reconciliation in Christ** (2 Cor 5:19 ESV): 2 Corinthians 5:19 states, "That is, in Christ God was reconciling the world to himself, not counting their trespasses against them,

and entrusting to us the message of reconciliation". This verse emphasizes the concept of reconciliation through Christ. Because of Adam's sin, human beings are the enemies of God. However, through the sacrificial death and resurrection of Jesus Christ, reconciliation between God and humanity was made possible. Jesus served as the mediator between God and humanity, bridging the gap and providing a way for people to be forgiven and restored to a right relationship with God. Through faith in Christ, individuals can experience the benefits of this reconciliation. Salvation, or the assurance of eternal life and forgiveness of sins, is secured by placing one's faith in Jesus Christ and accepting His atoning sacrifice. This reconciliation is a result of God's grace and His desire to reconcile humanity to Himself.

4. **Salvation is secure because of being born again in Christ** (John 3:3–5): Jesus tells Nicodemus that in order to see the kingdom of God, one must be "born again" or "born anew" (John 3:3–5). Being "born again" refers to a spiritual rebirth or regeneration that happens through faith in Jesus Christ. It is a transformation that takes place when a person acknowledges their need for the forgiveness of sins and accepts Jesus as their Savior and Lord. This new birth is not a physical one but a spiritual one, where the Holy Spirit comes to dwell within the believer and brings about a change in their heart and life. The concept of being "born again" emphasizes the need for a personal relationship with God through Jesus Christ. It is through this new birth and faith in Jesus that salvation is obtained. Salvation is the deliverance from the consequences of sin and the assurance of eternal life with God. It is secured by God's grace through faith, not by any personal efforts or good deeds (Eph. 2:8–9). Overall, being born again is a crucial aspect of Christian belief, representing the spiritual rebirth and transformation that leads to salvation through faith in Jesus Christ.

5. **Salvation is secure because it is the will of God in Christ** (John 6:39–40 NIV): "And this is the will of him who sent me, that I shall lose none of all those he has given me, but raise them up at the last day. For my Father's will is that everyone who looks to the Son and believes in him shall have eternal life, and I will raise them up at the last day" (John 6:39–40). In these verses, Jesus is speaking about the will of God concerning those who believe in Him. He assures that it is God's will

that none of those given to Him will be lost but will be raised up on the last day. This emphasizes the security of salvation for those who believe in Jesus. The passage teaches that the basis for this security lies in both the will of God and the faith and belief in Jesus as the Son of God. It is not dependent on our own efforts or works but on God's purpose and Jesus's redemptive work. Ultimately, the interpretation of this passage and the doctrine of salvation's security should be understood within the broader context of the entire Bible and in light of one's own faith tradition and beliefs.

6. **Salvation is secure because they shall never perish** (John 10:28–29 NIV): "I give them eternal life, and they shall never perish; no one will snatch them out of my hand. My Father, who has given them to me, is greater than all; no one can snatch them out of my Father's hand" (John 10:28–29). These words of Jesus express the security and assurance of salvation for those who believe in Him. Jesus promises that those who follow Him will receive eternal life and will never perish. He emphasizes the divine protection and care by stating that no one can snatch His followers out of His hand or the Father's hand. This passage highlights the concept of eternal security, often referred to as the perseverance of the saints. It asserts that once a person genuinely believes in Jesus Christ and places their faith in Him, they are eternally secure in their salvation. This verse highlights the security of salvation for believers in Jesus Christ, assuring them that they will never perish and that nothing can separate them from the love of God.

7. **Salvation is secure because Christ loves them to the end** (John 13:1 ESV): The verse, John 13:1, speaks of Jesus's love and its significance in the context of salvation. It says, "Now before the Feast of the Passover, when Jesus knew that his hour had come to depart out of this world to the Father, having loved his own who were in the world, he loved them to the end" (John 13:1). This verse highlights the depth and extent of Jesus's love for His followers. It signifies that Jesus's love is unwavering, enduring, and complete. It also points to the ultimate expression of His love, which was His sacrificial death on the cross. His love for humanity led Him to willingly offer Himself as a sacrifice to reconcile people with God and provide the way to eternal life. By accepting Jesus as their Lord and Savior, believers trust in His redemptive work and

find assurance that their salvation is secure. The verse emphasizes the profound love that Jesus demonstrated throughout His earthly ministry and ultimately in His death, underscoring the confidence believers have in their salvation through Him.

8. **Salvation is secure because Christ's sacrifice is once-for-all** (Heb. 10:10, 14): It is stated that Christ's sacrifice was offered once-for-all. This means that Jesus's sacrifice on the cross is seen as a complete and final atonement for the sins of humanity. Hebrews 10:10 says, "By that will we have been sanctified through the offering of the body of Jesus Christ once for all." This verse emphasizes the sanctifying power of Jesus's sacrifice and the idea that it was offered once and for all. Hebrews 10:14 further supports this by stating, "For by one offering He has perfected forever those who are being sanctified." This verse suggests that through Jesus's sacrifice, believers are made perfect, and their salvation is secure. The belief in the once-for-all sacrifice of Christ is rooted in the Christian doctrine of salvation. It teaches that through faith in Jesus and his sacrifice, believers receive forgiveness of sins and are reconciled with God. This salvation is considered permanent and cannot be earned or maintained through personal efforts or good works.

9. **Salvation is secure because God will remember our sin no more** (Heb. 10:17): The verse states, "Their sins and their lawless deeds I will remember no more." In the context of Hebrews, the author emphasizes the superiority of Christ's sacrifice over the sacrificial system of the Old Testament. The repeated animal sacrifices offered under the old covenant could never take away sins permanently. They were a reminder of sin year after year (Heb. 10:3–4). However, the sacrifice of Jesus on the cross was once-for-all, offering complete forgiveness and eternal redemption (Heb. 10:10–14). "God will remember our sin no more" means that through faith in Jesus Christ, God completely forgives and forgets our sins. This doesn't mean that God literally forgets or loses memory of our past transgressions. Instead, it signifies that God chooses not to hold our sins against us or bring them up in judgment. It is an expression of His mercy and grace. This verse provides assurance to believers that their salvation is secure.

10. **Salvation is secure because He always lives to make intercession for them** (Heb. 7:25): The verse states, "Therefore He is also able to save the uttermost those who come to God through Him, since He always lives to make intercession for them." This verse highlights the role of Jesus Christ as our advocate and mediator before God. The phrase "able to save completely" emphasizes the sufficiency and effectiveness of Christ's work on the cross. Through his sacrificial death and resurrection, Jesus has provided salvation for all who put their trust in him. Furthermore, the verse emphasizes that Jesus "always lives to intercede" for believers. This means that even after his resurrection and ascension to heaven, Jesus continues to be actively involved in the lives of his followers. He intercedes on their behalf, advocating for them before God, and ensuring their security in salvation. The intercession of Christ provides believers with confidence and assurance. It assures us that our salvation is not dependent on our own efforts or merits but rests securely in the work and advocacy of Jesus. His continuous intercession strengthens our faith and reminds us that our relationship with God is secure.

11. **Salvation is secure because the believer is righteous before God** (2 Cor. 5:21 NIV): The verse says, "God made him who had no sin to be sin for us so that in him we might become the righteousness of God." According to Christian belief, salvation is attained through faith in Jesus Christ. It explains that Jesus, who was without sin, took upon himself the sins of humanity. Through this act, believers are considered righteous before God. This righteousness is not something believers achieve through their own efforts but is imputed or credited to them through their faith in Jesus. Justification refers to being declared righteous by God through faith in Jesus Christ. This righteousness is based on the atoning work of Christ. It is important to note that this justification is received by grace through faith and not by any merit of our own. We hold that once a person is justified by faith in Christ, their salvation is secure and cannot be lost. This perspective is often rooted in the understanding that salvation is a gift from God and not something that can be earned or forfeited through human actions.

12. **Salvation is secure because we will never thirst again** (John 4:13–14 NIV): "Jesus answered, 'Everyone who drinks this water will be thirsty again, but whoever drinks the water I give them will never thirst. Indeed,

the water I give them will become in them a spring of water welling up to eternal life'" (John 4:13–14). In this conversation, Jesus uses water as a metaphor to illustrate a spiritual truth. He contrasts physical water, which only temporarily satisfies thirst and requires repeated consumption, with the spiritual water He offers, which brings eternal satisfaction and life. When Jesus speaks of never thirsting again, He is referring to the spiritual satisfaction and eternal life that come through faith in Him. He offers a deep and lasting fulfillment that extends beyond our physical needs and desires. In other words, He provides a spiritual refreshment and nourishment that satisfies the deepest longings of our hearts. Regarding salvation, the Bible teaches that faith in Jesus Christ is the means by which we receive eternal life and have our sins forgiven. When we place our trust in Him, we are reconciled with God and receive the gift of salvation. This salvation is described as secure because it is based on God's grace and the finished work of Jesus on the cross rather than on our own efforts or abilities.

13. **Salvation is secure because we are the body of Christ** (Col. 1:18 NIV): Christ as the head of believers is of paramount importance for the assurance of salvation. Christ's role as the head of the church and the Savior of humanity is a central tenet of Christian faith. Colossians 1:18 states, "And he is the head of the body, the church; he is the beginning and the firstborn from among the dead so that in everything he might have the supremacy." This verse emphasizes the preeminence of Christ as the head of the church, which is often referred to as the body of Christ. The concept of the body of Christ is a metaphorical expression used in the New Testament to describe the collective unity of believers in Jesus Christ. Just as a human body has many parts functioning together, Christians are considered members of the body of Christ, with Christ as the head. The assurance of salvation comes from the trust and reliance placed in Christ as the head. It is through Him that believers have access to God, receive forgiveness of sins, and are granted eternal life.

14. **Salvation is secure because Christ is the bridegroom of a believer** (Mark 10:7–8 NIV): Mark 10:7–8 says, "For this reason, a man will leave his father and mother and be united to his wife, and the two will become one flesh." Jesus quotes these verses when discussing divorce

and emphasizes the lifelong commitment of marriage. The concept of Christ as the Bridegroom is more extensively explored in other passages of the New Testament, such as Ephesians 5:25–27 and Revelation 19:7–9. In these verses, the relationship between Christ and the church (believers) is likened to that of a husband and wife, symbolizing the intimate and eternal bond between Christ and His followers. The context of this passage is primarily focused on the sanctity and permanence of marriage. Jesus is emphasizing that when a man and a woman are joined in marriage, they become one in a profound and intimate way. It signifies a union that is not easily broken. In this metaphorical sense, the unity and oneness between a husband and wife can serve as an illustration of the profound spiritual unity that believers have with Christ. The believers' relationship with Christ is meant to be intimate, devoted, and inseparable.

15. **Salvation is secure because we are fully saved by Christ** (Isa. 53:6 NIV; 1 John 1:7b NIV): The statement reflects a Christian belief regarding salvation through faith in Jesus Christ. Isaiah 53:6 and 1 John 1:7b are verses from the Bible that are often interpreted to support the idea that salvation is secured through Christ. Isaiah 53:6 states, "We all, like sheep, have gone astray, each of us has turned to our own way; and the Lord has laid on him the iniquity of us all." This verse is considered a prophecy in the Hebrew Bible that Christians believe refers to Jesus's sacrificial death on the cross, taking upon himself the sins of humanity. According to this belief, through faith in Jesus and accepting his sacrifice, individuals can be saved from the consequences of sin. 1 John 1:7b says, "The blood of Jesus, his Son, cleanses us from all sin." Christians interpret this verse to emphasize the cleansing power of Jesus's blood, which brings forgiveness and redemption. It is through faith in Jesus and his atoning work that believers are purified and saved. We emphasize that salvation is a gift of God's grace and is secured through faith in Jesus Christ.

16. **Salvation is secure because it is the works of the Holy Spirit** (John 16:8): The verse states: "And when He come, He will convict the world of sin, and of righteousness, and of judgement." Here, Jesus is explaining that the Holy Spirit will convict and guide people in recognizing their sinfulness, the righteousness of God, and the impending judgment. The

Bible teaches that salvation is by grace through faith in Jesus Christ (Eph. 2:8–9). It is a result of God's love and mercy, demonstrated through the sacrificial death and resurrection of Jesus Christ. The Holy Spirit's work in the process of salvation includes convicting individuals of their need for a Savior, illuminating the truth of the gospel, and empowering believers to live a transformed life. The Holy Spirit enables believers to have faith in Christ and empowers them to live according to God's will. It requires a personal response of faith and repentance from individuals. The Bible teaches that we must believe in our hearts and confess with our mouths that Jesus is Lord in order to be saved (Rom. 10:9–10). In salvation, God initiates, enables, and offers salvation, but we must respond in faith.

17. **Salvation is secure because of our relationship with Christ** (1 Cor. 15:22 NIV): It is true that our relationship with Christ is essential for salvation. 1 Corinthians 15:22 states, "For as in Adam all die, so in Christ, all will be made alive." This verse is part of a larger passage in which the apostle Paul discusses the resurrection of the dead. He explains that through Adam, the first man, death entered the world, bringing about the physical and spiritual death of all humanity. However, through Christ, all believers will be raised to life again. The verse emphasizes the redemptive work of Christ. Through His sacrificial death and subsequent resurrection, He has provided a way for humanity to experience eternal life. By having faith in Jesus and accepting Him as our Savior, we can partake in this resurrection and receive salvation. Our relationship with Christ is indeed crucial for salvation. It is by God's grace, expressed through Jesus Christ, that our salvation is made secure. It's important to note that our relationship with Christ is perfect and eternal, but fellowship with Him involves continuing to grow in our faith, seeking to live according to His teachings, and relying on His grace.

18. **Salvation is secure because a believer has the Son, Jesus Christ** (1 John 5:12–13 NIV): "Whoever has the Son has life; whoever does not have the Son of God does not have life. I write these things to you who believe in the name of the Son of God so that you may know that you have eternal life." These verses affirm that those who have received and accepted Jesus Christ, the Son of God, into their lives have eternal life.

They possess a relationship with Him, and as a result, they have the assurance of salvation. Jesus Christ, through His life, death, and resurrection, offers salvation to all who believe in Him. When a person places their faith in Jesus and accepts Him as their Lord and Savior, they are united with Him spiritually. This union grants them forgiveness of sins, reconciliation with God, and the gift of eternal life. The assurance of salvation comes from the unchanging nature of God's promise. Believers can find confidence in their salvation because it is not based on their own efforts or merits but on the finished work of Jesus Christ. Those who have placed their faith in Jesus Christ can have the assurance of salvation. Their confidence rests in the fact that they have the son and therefore possess eternal life.

19. Salvation is secure because your life is hidden with Christ in God (Col. 3:3): Colossians 3:3 indeed states, "For you died, and your life is hidden with Christ in God." This verse conveys an important aspect of the Christian faith regarding salvation and the believer's relationship with Jesus Christ. The phrase "your life is hidden with Christ in God" points to the concept of the believer's identity and security being rooted in Christ. It signifies that when a person accepts Jesus Christ as their Savior and follows Him, their old self, characterized by sin and separation from God, has died. Through faith, they are united with Christ, and their new life is intricately connected with Him. This verse emphasizes the security of salvation for believers. It implies that since their life is hidden with Christ in God, God's power protects and preserves it. This assurance rests not on their own efforts or merits but on their union with Christ. As a result, believers can have confidence in their eternal destiny and the faithfulness of God to keep them secure. The foundation of salvation and the believer's ultimate security lie in their union with Christ and the work He has accomplished on their behalf.

20. Salvation is secure because a believer is a child of God (Rom. 8:15): Romans 8:15 says, "For you did not receive the spirit of bondage again to fear, but you received the Spirit of adoption by whom we cry out, 'Abba! Father!'" In these verses, the apostle Paul is emphasizing the transformation that takes place when a person becomes a believer in Jesus Christ. Through faith, believers receive the Holy Spirit, who is referred to as the Spirit of adoption. This adoption into God's family is not based on human efforts or works but is a result of God's grace and the believer's faith in Jesus. As children of God, believers experience a new relationship with Him. They are no longer in bondage or fear but have the privilege of calling God their Father, using the intimate term "Abba." This demonstrates the closeness and security believers have in their relationship with God. Furthermore, the Holy Spirit bears witness with our spirit that we are indeed children of God. This internal witness provides believers with assurance and confidence in their salvation. It is the Holy Spirit affirming and assuring believers that they belong to God's family. Once someone becomes a child of God, they are eternally secure in their relationship with Him.

21. **Salvation is secure because we have received eternal inheritance (Heb. 9:15):** Hebrews 9:15 states, "And for this reason He is the Mediator of the new covenant, by means of death, for the redemption of the transgressions under the first covenant, that those who are called may receive the promise of the eternal inheritance." This verse emphasizes the role of Jesus Christ as the mediator of a new covenant, which brings about the promised eternal inheritance for those who are called. The new covenant, which was established through Jesus's death and resurrection, offers forgiveness and redemption from the transgressions committed under the old covenant. According to Christian doctrine, salvation is a gift from God that is received through faith in Jesus Christ. This gift includes the forgiveness of sins, reconciliation with God, and the promise of eternal life with Him. The new covenant, established through Jesus's sacrificial death, provides a once-for-all redemption and an eternal inheritance for those who believe in Him. By receiving this eternal inheritance through faith in Jesus Christ, believers can have confidence in their salvation. The eternal inheritance assures believers of their future with God, where they will experience His presence, love, and blessings for all eternity.

22. **Salvation is secure because a believer has passed from death into life (John 5:24 ESV):** John 5:24 says, "Truly, truly, I say to you, whoever hears my word and believes him who sent me has eternal life. He does not come into judgment but has passed from death to life". This verse is often understood in the context of salvation and the assurance of eternal life for believers in Jesus Christ. It emphasizes the

transformative nature of faith in Christ and the security that comes with it. According to this verse, Jesus states that those who hear His Word and believe in the One who sent Him (God the Father) have eternal life. This belief is not merely intellectual assent but an active trust and reliance on Jesus as the Son of God and the Savior. Such individuals are said to have "passed from death to life." This transition refers to a spiritual rebirth or regeneration that takes place when a person becomes a believer in Christ. It signifies a new spiritual existence and a restored relationship with God. The verse also highlights the assurance and security that believers possess. It states that they "do not come into judgment." This does not mean that believers will never face any consequences or evaluations of their actions, but rather that they are saved from the ultimate judgment of eternal separation from God. Instead, they receive the gift of eternal life.

23. **Salvation is secure because Christ lives in the believer** (Rev. 3:20; Col. 1:27): Revelation 3:20 states, "Behold, I stand at the door and knock. If anyone hears My voice and opens the door, I will come in to him and dine with him, and he with Me." This verse is often interpreted as Jesus speaking to believers, inviting them to have a personal relationship with Him. It emphasizes the idea of inviting Jesus into one's life and having fellowship with Him. Colossians 1:27 says, "To them God willed to make known what are the riches of the glory of this mystery among the Gentiles: which is Christ in you, the hope of glory." This verse highlights the concept that Christ dwells within believers, referring to the presence of the Holy Spirit within those who have accepted Jesus as their Savior. It conveys the notion that through faith in Christ, believers have a hope of experiencing the glory of God. Based on these verses, Christians believe in the doctrine of "eternal security" or "once saved, always saved," which suggests that once a person has genuinely accepted Jesus as their Savior, their salvation is secure and cannot be lost. This perspective asserts that because Christ lives within believers, they are eternally secure in their salvation.

24. **Salvation is secure because nothing can separate us from the love of God** (Rom. 8:35 NIV): It speaks to the security of salvation and the unwavering love of God. It says, "Who shall separate us from the love of Christ? Shall trouble or hardship or persecution or famine or

nakedness or danger or sword?" This verse emphasizes the assurance that believers have in their salvation. It declares that nothing in all of creation has the power to separate us from the love of God that is found in Christ Jesus. The apostle Paul, who wrote the book of Romans, presents a list of potential hardships and challenges that one might face in life, and he asserts that none of them can separate us from God's love. This verse provides great comfort and reassurance to Christians, reminding them that their salvation is secure and that no external circumstances or difficulties can separate them from the love and grace of God. It affirms that God's love is unconditional and unchanging, extending to believers regardless of their circumstances. It is important to note that while this verse speaks of the security of salvation, it does not mean that believers are exempt from facing challenges or difficulties in life. Rather, it assures them that even in the midst of hardships, they can have confidence in the unending love of God and the eternal security of their salvation.

This assurance should not lead to complacency but should inspire believers to live in a manner consistent with their faith. It's important to note that the security of salvation does not imply that a person can live however they please without regard for God's commands. Genuine faith in Christ leads to a transformed life and a desire to follow Him. The assurance of salvation is not a license for willful and unrepentant sin but rather a confidence in God's faithfulness and the power of Christ's sacrifice. The Bible also teaches the importance of living a life of obedience and holiness (Rom. 6:1–4; 1 John 2:3–6).

30. WHEN WE COMMIT SIN AFTER BEING SAVED

The Bible acknowledges the possibility of believers committing sins, but it also emphasizes the provision that has been made for our eternal forgiveness. When believers sin, we can confess our sins, repent, and seek forgiveness through Jesus. By doing so, we can be restored to a right relationship with God. It's important to note that while Christians strive to live a life that is pleasing to God and to avoid sin, we recognize our ongoing need for God's grace and forgiveness. We seek to grow in our faith and rely on the Holy Spirit to empower us to resist temptation and live in accordance with the Scriptures.

WHEN WE COMMIT SIN, WHAT SHOULD WE DO?

1. **Confess our sins:** (1 John 1:8) When Christians commit sin, the Bible emphasizes the importance of confession and repentance. It is acknowledged that claiming to be without sin is self-deception, emphasizing the ongoing struggle with sin even after spiritual rebirth. While salvation through Jesus Christ offers forgiveness for past, present, and future sins, it does not grant believers a license to continue sinning without consequences. The transformative power of the Holy Spirit enables Christians to resist temptation and pursue righteousness, but when sins occur, acknowledging them, repenting, and seeking forgiveness from God are crucial steps. Christians recognize their inherent fallibility, aiming to live a life free from sin while growing in faith and becoming more Christlike through the continuous influence of the Holy Spirit.

2. **We have an Advocate:** (1 John 2:1) The Christian doctrine of salvation assures believers that through faith in Jesus Christ, our sins are forgiven upon spiritual rebirth. However, this does not exempt Christians from future sin. Believers are reminded that even after being born again, they may still sin due to their human nature and the presence of temptation. The passage introduces the concept of Jesus Christ serving as an Advocate or mediator before God the Father. This means that when believers do sin, we can turn to Jesus, confess our sins, repent, and seek forgiveness, thereby restoring our relationship with God. The assurance of having an Advocate underscores the ongoing grace and forgiveness available to Christians as we navigate the challenges of living a righteous life in a fallen world.

3. **Forsake our sins:** (John 5:14) Jesus tells a healed man to "sin no more" after spiritual transformation, emphasizing the importance of turning away from sin. Being "born again" for Christians means a new life in Christ, aligning with God's will. Despite this, human mistakes may lead to sin, but persisting without repentance can harm spiritual well-being. The verse warns of detrimental effects and urges believers to actively avoid sin, emphasizing the need to confess, repent, seek forgiveness, and continually strive to live in accordance with God's commandments.

IF WE COMMIT SIN, OUR SALVATION WILL NOT BE LOST, BUT ...

1. **We may grieve the Holy Spirit:** Ephesians 4:30 warns believers not to grieve the Holy Spirit, urging us to avoid behaviors contrary to God's nature, such as disobedience and slander. While the verse doesn't imply the Holy Spirit departs when believers sin, it emphasizes the importance of living in alignment with God's will to nurture a close relationship with the Holy Spirit. Engaging in sinful actions can hinder spiritual growth and quench the Holy Spirit's work in one's life.

2. **We may lose our joy:** Psalm 51:12 expresses King David's plea for the restoration of joy after confessing his sins. Although salvation is a gift received through faith in Jesus Christ, unconfessed sin can impact fellowship with God, affecting joy and peace. While salvation remains secure, restoring fellowship involves confession, repentance, and seeking forgiveness. David's prayer highlights the desire to regain the joy that comes from a right relationship with God, emphasizing the role of repentance in experiencing the fullness of joy and peace.

3. **We may lose our fellowship with God:** 1 John 1:7b–10 discusses sin, fellowship, and our relationship with God. While sin can disrupt our temporal fellowship with God, the eternal relationship remains secure through Jesus's sacrifice. Maintaining honesty, confessing sins, and aligning with God's truth are crucial for ongoing fellowship. The eternal relationship is based on Jesus's work, securing salvation, and characterized by forgiveness. Temporal fellowship involves ongoing interactions among believers, requiring confession, repentance, and restoration when sins occur. Both aspects contribute to Christian growth and well-being.

4. **We may be disciplined by God:** Hebrews 12:5-8 emphasizes God's loving discipline towards His children, portraying it as a sign of His love and acceptance. The purpose of God's discipline is correction and training, not rejection. Committing sin doesn't mean losing one's relationship with God but serves as a reminder of His care, guiding believers away from harmful behaviors and towards a life aligned with His will.

5. **We may not be utilized by God:** 2 Timothy 2:20-21 highlights the idea that individuals who cleanse themselves from dishonorable actions can be used by God for honorable purposes. It underscores personal purity and living according to God's standards. While salvation is a gift received through faith in Jesus Christ and not earned through good deeds, maintaining a life in alignment with God's standards enables effective service to Him, though salvation itself remains secure.

6. **We may lose our reward:** In 1 Corinthians 3:15, Paul distinguishes between salvation and rewards, explaining that believers' works will be tested. While salvation is secure through faith in Jesus Christ, varying degrees of heavenly rewards are based on believers' faithfulness and the quality of our works. Loss of rewards does not affect salvation, as it is a gift of God's grace and mercy.

7. **Our deadly sin may result in physical death:** 1 Corinthians 5:1-5 addresses a case of severe sexual immorality in the Corinthian church, cautioning against broad generalizations about every sin leading to physical death for born-again believers. The passage emphasizes the need for disciplinary action within the church community. The concept of being "born again" signifies spiritual transformation through accepting Jesus as Lord and Savior, involving reconciliation with God, forgiveness, and empowerment by the Holy Spirit for a God-honoring life. Salvation is a result of God's grace and accepting Jesus, not earned by avoiding sin. While sin impacts relationships, salvation depends on faith in Jesus for forgiveness and eternal life with God.

When we commit sin after being saved, it is important to understand that our salvation is not dependent on our ability to live a sinless life. Salvation is a gift from God, given through faith in Jesus Christ, and is based on His grace, not our works (Eph. 2:8-9). However, sin does have consequences, even for believers as mentioned above. God has provided a way for us to be restored when we do sin. It is essential to repent, seek forgiveness, and rely on the Holy Spirit to help us overcome sin and grow in our walk with Christ.

31. JESUS, ONE WAY

For billions of individuals worldwide, Christ is not just a historical figure but a spiritual beacon of hope and salvation. The belief that Jesus is the only way to salvation is a central tenet in Christianity, shaping the faith's core doctrines and guiding the lives of its adherents. This notion asserts that through His sacrificial death and resurrection, Jesus offers humanity the exclusive path to eternal redemption and reconciliation with God. In this essay, we will delve into the theological underpinnings of this belief, examining its significance, implications, and enduring relevance in contemporary society.

1. **Because His name is Jesus (Yahshua), which means "God Saves"** (Matt. 1:21): The belief that Jesus is the only way for salvation is a central tenet of Christianity. In Matthew 1:21, an angel appears to Joseph in a dream and says, "And she will bring forth a Son, and you shall call His name JESUS, for He will save His people from their sins." This verse highlights the belief among Christians that Jesus's purpose was to bring salvation to humanity. According to Christian theology, Jesus is seen as the Son of God and the Savior of mankind. His death on the cross is believed to have provided atonement for the sins of humanity, making salvation possible.

2. **Because of His virgin birth, He is sinless and qualified for the Savior** (Isa. 7:14): Jesus's virgin birth is seen as an essential aspect of His sinlessness and qualification to be the Savior. The concept of Jesus's sinlessness stems from the belief that all human beings inherit a sinful nature from Adam. However, Jesus, being born of a virgin, is to have been conceived by the Holy Spirit and not through human descent. This unique birth is considered significant because it means Jesus was not subject to the sinful nature inherited by other humans. Jesus's sinless nature made Him the only qualified Savior.

3. **Because Jesus is the only one who descended from heaven and ascended** (John 3:13 NIV; Acts 1:9): Jesus is seen as the Son of God who came down from heaven to earth, lived a sinless life, and sacrificed Himself on the cross to provide salvation for humanity. John

3:13 states, "No one has ever gone into heaven except the one who came from heaven—the Son of Man." In this verse, Jesus is speaking to Nicodemus about the authority and uniqueness of His teachings. Acts 1:9 describes the moment of Jesus's ascension after His resurrection. This verse affirms Jesus's heavenly origin and return. For these reasons, He only knows how to get to heaven.

4. **Because Jesus is the only one who takes away the sins of the world** (John 1:29): The statement you've mentioned reflects a particular belief held by Christians that Jesus is the only way to salvation. According to this belief, Jesus is considered the ultimate sacrifice who takes upon himself the sins of the world. John 1:29 states, "The next day John saw Jesus coming toward him, and said, 'Behold, the Lamb of God, who takes away the sin of the world!'" In this verse, John the Baptist refers to Jesus as the Lamb of God, symbolizing his sacrificial role in taking away the sins of humanity.

5. **Because Jesus is the only one who shed His blood for our forgiveness of sin** (Heb. 9:22): It states, "And according to the law almost all things are purified with blood, and without shedding of blood there is no remission." This verse is often interpreted to emphasize the importance of Jesus's sacrificial death and the shedding of his blood as the means by which forgiveness of sins is obtained. All humans are sinners and separated from God, and Jesus's sacrifice on the cross provided a way for reconciliation with God. Through faith in Jesus and acceptance of his sacrifice, believers can receive forgiveness for their sins and be reconciled with God, leading to salvation and eternal life.

6. **Because Jesus is the only gate and way to get to heaven** (John 10:9; 14:6): In John 10:9, Jesus says, "I am the door. If anyone enters by Me, he will be saved and will go in and out and find pasture." This metaphorical statement implies that Jesus is the means through which people can access salvation and find spiritual nourishment. Similarly, in John 14:6, Jesus declares, "I am the way, the truth, and the life. No one comes to the Father except through Me." Here, Jesus is claiming that He alone provides the path to eternal life and a relationship with God the Father. Jesus Christ is the exclusive mediator between humanity and God.

THE WAY OF SALVATION

7. **Because Jesus is the only sinless Person who can make us righteous before God** (2 Cor. 5:21 ESV): The belief that Jesus is the only way for salvation is a perspective held by many Christians and is rooted in their interpretation of biblical teachings. According to Christian doctrine, Jesus is considered the Son of God and the Savior of humanity. It states, "For our sake, he made him to be sin who knew no sin, so that in him we might become the righteousness of God." This verse highlights that Jesus, being sinless, took upon himself the sins of humanity and, through his sacrifice, offers salvation and righteousness to those who believe in him.

8. **Because Jesus is the only Person who is resurrected from death to life** (John 11:25–26): The resurrection of Jesus Christ is considered a central event in human history and a demonstration of His divinity and power over death. Christianity teaches that Jesus, as the Son of God, willingly died on the cross to atone for the sins of humanity. His resurrection, which occurred three days after His crucifixion, is seen as a triumph over sin and death. A dead god cannot save us. Through faith in Jesus and His sacrifice, Christians believe they can receive forgiveness for their sins and have eternal life.

9. **Because only Jesus can be the Mediator between God and men** (1 Tim. 2:5–6): It says, "For there is one God and one Mediator between God and men, the Man Christ Jesus, who gave Himself as a ransom for all, to be testified in due time." This verse emphasizes the unique role of Jesus Christ as the mediator between God and humanity. In Christian theology, the belief is that Jesus is the Son of God who came to earth in human form, lived a sinless life, and sacrificed Himself on the cross to reconcile humanity with God. The concept of salvation through Jesus is rooted in the belief that His sacrificial death and resurrection provided a way for people to be forgiven of their sins and have a restored relationship with God.

10. **Because only the one who has the Son (Jesus) has eternal life** (1 John 5:12 NIV; Rev. 3:20): Jesus is the Son of God and the Savior of humanity. Christians believe that through his life, death, and resurrection, Jesus offers forgiveness of sins and the promise of eternal life to those who have faith in him. In 1 John 5:12, it states, "Whoever has

the Son has life; whoever does not have the Son of God does not have life." This verse suggests that having a personal relationship with Jesus is essential for obtaining eternal life. Revelation 3:20 is often interpreted as an invitation for individuals to accept Jesus into their lives and experience salvation through him.

11. **Because Jesus sent the Holy Spirit to be sure of our salvation** (John 16:8): "And when He has come, He will convict the world of sin, and of righteousness, and of judgement." This verse is part of Jesus's teaching to his disciples about the coming of the Holy Spirit. It suggests that the Holy Spirit will convict and guide people regarding sin, righteousness, and judgment. Christians interpret this as the Holy Spirit's role in helping individuals recognize their need for salvation and understand God's standard of righteousness. It signifies the presence of the Holy Spirit in the lives of believers, providing assurance and serving as a reminder of their future redemption and eternal inheritance.

12. **Because only through Jesus a believer has passed from death into life** (John 5:24): It says, "Most assuredly, I say to you, he who hears My word and believes in Him who sent Me has everlasting life, and shall not come into judgement, but has passed from death into life." This verse is attributed to Jesus, who is the Son of God and the Savior of humanity. The verse highlights the importance of faith in Jesus and believing in God, as stated by Jesus Himself. According to this verse, those who hear the Word of Jesus and believe in God, the One who sent Him, are promised eternal life and are said to have "passed from death into life."

13. **Because Jesus Christ Himself lives in the believer** (Col. 1:27): The concept of Christ living within believers is often associated with the Christian doctrine of the Holy Spirit. When individuals accept Jesus Christ as their Lord and Savior, they receive the Holy Spirit, who indwells them and guides them in their spiritual journey. This indwelling presence of Christ through the Holy Spirit is essential for salvation. It is important to note that the belief that Jesus is the only way to salvation and that He lives within believers is a core tenet of Christian faith: at Christmas, "God with us," at Calvary, "God for us," and at Pentecost, "God in us."

14. **Because a believer becomes a member of the body of Christ** (1 Cor. 12:13–14): It speaks about believers becoming the body of Christ. In this context, the apostle Paul is emphasizing the unity and diversity within the Christian community. He uses the metaphor of the body to illustrate that just as a human body has many different parts with different functions, the members of the Christian community have different spiritual gifts and roles, but they are all united in Christ. According to the Bible, the believers are the body of Christ, and Christ is the Head of all believers.

> Charles H. Spurgeon writes, "Every believer is a member of Christ's body. If you will only grant me my head afloat above the water, I will give you permission to drown my fingers. Try it, you cannot do it. Christ, the head of the body, is in heaven, and until you can drown the head of the body, you cannot drown the body. And if the head be in heaven and beyond the reach of harm, then every member of the body is alive and secure, and shall at last be in heaven too" (Carter 1988, 185).[20]

In conclusion, the concept of Jesus as the only way to salvation holds a profound place in the hearts and minds of countless individuals across the globe. Rooted in the core teachings of Christianity, this belief encapsulates the central message of Christ's life: love, forgiveness, and divine redemption. For believers, the acceptance of Jesus as their Savior brings solace and reassurance, affirming the promise of eternal life and communion with God. How can a believer perish if he is a member of Christ's body?

32. OLD TESTAMENT PEOPLE

According to Christian beliefs, Jesus Christ is seen as the unique and definitive Savior, who offers salvation and reconciliation with God to humanity through his life, death, and resurrection. However, it is important to note that the understanding of salvation and the role of Jesus Christ has evolved over time. How could unbelievers who lived prior to AD 33 logically be saved by Christ who had not yet offered Himself as a sacrifice for our sins? In the Old Testament, prior to the birth of Jesus, people's relationship with God was primarily based on their faith and obedience to God's commands.

The Assurance of Salvation

1. Some Important Points for OT Salvation

1) Covenant Relationship Was by Faith: In the Old Testament, salvation was often understood in terms of a covenant relationship with God. God established covenants with individuals and the Israelite community as a whole, offering them the opportunity for a relationship with Him and His blessings. One of the key examples is the covenant established with Abraham in Genesis 15:6, which says, "And he believed in the LORD, and He accounted it to him for righteousness." This verse emphasizes that Abraham's faith in God's promises resulted in righteousness being credited to him. In the Old Testament, people were saved by placing their faith in God, obeying His commands, and seeking forgiveness for their sins through various means, such as offering sacrifices. The sacrificial system, outlined in the books of Leviticus and Deuteronomy, provided a means for people to approach God and find forgiveness for their transgressions. The shedding of animal blood in sacrificial offerings symbolized the atonement and forgiveness of sins.

2) The Cross: The New Testament provides further insights into the relationship between the Old Testament and Jesus's redemptive work. In John 8:56–59, Jesus refers to Abraham's joy at seeing His day, suggesting that Abraham had some knowledge or anticipation of Jesus's coming and the salvation He would bring. Jesus's sacrifice on the cross is considered the ultimate atonement for the sins of humanity, fulfilling the sacrificial system of the Old Testament. In John 19:30, Jesus's words, "It is finished," indicate the completion of His redemptive work through His death and resurrection. This event marked the fulfillment of God's plan for salvation and opened the way for all people, in the past and the future, to be saved through faith in Jesus Christ.

3) Only through Christ: Isaiah 53:6 is a prophetic passage that describes the suffering servant who would bear the sins of many. This passage is often seen as a foreshadowing of Jesus Christ and his sacrificial death on the cross for the forgiveness of sins. In John 8:56–59, Jesus refers to himself in relation to Abraham, saying, "Before Abraham was born, I am." This statement implies Jesus's

eternal existence and divine nature. Jesus's claim to be the "I am" echoes the name of God revealed to Moses in Exodus 3:14. Jesus's sacrifice on the cross and his resurrection made salvation available to all who believe in him.

4) No Limit for Mercy and Grace: While Jesus Christ is the ultimate way to salvation in Christian theology, it is also important to recognize that God's mercy and grace are not limited by time or space. God's plan for salvation encompasses the past and future, extending beyond specific historical events. The means by which individuals were saved before the birth of Jesus Christ is a topic of theological debate, but many Christians believe that those who lived before Christ could still be saved through their faith and relationship with God.

2. **Looking Forward and Looking Backward to Calvary:** In the Old Testament, the people of Israel anticipated the coming of the Messiah who would bring salvation. They looked forward to the promised deliverance and restoration, which included forgiveness of sins and a renewed relationship with God. Many prophecies in the Old Testament pointed toward the coming of a Messiah, such as Isaiah 53 and Micah 5:2. In the New Testament, Jesus Christ is revealed as the fulfillment of those prophecies. The birth, life, death, and resurrection of Jesus are understood as the climax of God's redemptive plan. Therefore, New Testament believers look backward to the historical event of Jesus's crucifixion and resurrection, recognizing it as the definitive act of salvation accomplished by Christ.

3. **Old Testament People Were Saved on Credit:** Robert Jeffress says, "During the time period before Christ died, I like to say that people were saved on credit" (Jeffress 2016, 164).[21]
The statement is a metaphorical way of expressing that their salvation was based on faith and anticipation of what God would do in the future through the coming Messiah. In other words, they believed in God's promises and trusted that He would provide a way of salvation. Old Testament figures, such as Abraham, Moses, David, and the prophets, demonstrated faith in God's promises and trusted in His righteousness. They looked forward to the coming of the Messiah and believed that

God would save them based on their faith and obedience to His commandments. Their faith and righteousness, however, did not provide complete forgiveness of sins but served as a temporary covering until the ultimate sacrifice of Christ on the cross.

The sacrificial system in the Old Testament, including the offering of animal sacrifices, served as a temporary means of atonement, pointing to the future sacrifice of Christ. It was through faith in God and the anticipation of the coming Messiah that Old Testament believers found salvation. Their faith and righteousness were accounted to them as righteousness (Gen. 15:6), but the complete forgiveness of sins and eternal salvation were ultimately accomplished through Jesus' sacrifice on the cross. The salvation of Old Testament believers was based on faith and anticipation of God's promises, while the sacrifice of Jesus on the cross provided the ultimate and complete salvation for all who believe in Him.

33. SALVATION AND REWARDS

The concept of salvation and rewards holds significant importance in the Bible, encompassing the promises and blessings bestowed upon believers by God. These intertwined themes are central to the Christian faith, offering hope, assurance, and motivation for living a life aligned with God's will. In this exploration, we will delve into the biblical teachings on salvation and rewards, examining the profound implications they hold for believers and their eternal destiny.

1. **Salvation:** At the core of Christianity lies the doctrine of salvation, which embodies the profound truth that God, in His infinite love and mercy, offers redemption and eternal life to humanity. The Bible teaches that all people are sinners and fall short of God's perfect standards. Yet, in His grace, God sent His Son, Jesus Christ, to bear the weight of humanity's sins on the cross. Through faith in Jesus's sacrificial death and resurrection, individuals can receive forgiveness and be reconciled with God. Salvation is not merely an abstract concept but a transformative experience. It involves a personal relationship with God, whereby believers are born anew and become partakers of God's divine nature. This spiritual rebirth brings about a restoration of fellowship

with the Creator, enabling believers to experience His love, peace, and joy. Moreover, salvation assures believers of their eternal destiny in the presence of God, free from the power and penalty of sin.

2. **Rewards:** While salvation is a gift freely offered to all who believe, the Bible also speaks of rewards that await believers in the life to come. These rewards, bestowed by God's grace, are not means to earn salvation but rather a demonstration of God's generosity and faithfulness toward His children. They serve as an incentive for believers to live faithfully, obediently, and wholeheartedly in this present life. The Scriptures depict various types of rewards that believers can anticipate. These include the crown of life, the crown of righteousness, the imperishable crown, and the crown of glory, among others. These symbolic crowns signify the blessings, honors, and privileges reserved for those who faithfully follow Christ and persevere in their faith. Moreover, rewards can also encompass the joy of hearing God's words of affirmation, "Well done, good and faithful servant." Importantly, rewards are not an expression of God's favoritism or a means of comparison among believers. Rather, they reflect God's perfect justice and His acknowledgment of the efforts, sacrifices, and faithfulness demonstrated by individuals in their earthly lives. They serve as an encouragement to live with a heavenly perspective, investing in eternal values rather than temporal pursuits.

3. **The Difference between Salvation and Rewards**

   1) Salvation Is a Gift (Rom. 6: 23b): It says, "But the gift of God is eternal life in Christ Jesus our Lord." This verse emphasizes that salvation, specifically eternal life, is a gift from God. It cannot be earned or obtained through our own efforts or good works. It is freely given to us through faith in Jesus Christ. This verse emphasizes the grace and mercy of God, who offers salvation as a gift to all who believe in Him.

      Reward Is Earned (Matt. 10:42 NIV): It says, "And if anyone gives even a cup of cold water to one of these little ones who is my disciple, truly I tell you, that person will certainly not lose their reward." This verse speaks about rewards that are earned through acts of kindness and service done in the name of Jesus. It highlights the idea that when we demonstrate love and compassion to others, especially to those who belong to Christ, there is a reward that awaits us.

2) Salvation Is for the Lost Sinners: The Bible teaches that all human beings are sinners and separated from God because of their sinful nature and actions. However, God, out of His love and mercy, offers salvation as a means of reconciliation and forgiveness. According to Christian belief, salvation is obtained through faith in Jesus Christ as the Son of God and Savior, who sacrificed Himself on the cross to pay for humanity's sins. Through belief in Jesus and acceptance of His sacrifice, individuals can receive salvation and be reconciled with God.

Reward Is for the Children of God: The Bible also speaks about rewards for those who follow God faithfully and live according to His teachings. While salvation is a free gift available to all, rewards are often associated with believers' actions, obedience, and service to God. These rewards are seen as blessings and inheritances in the life to come. Rewards, on the other hand, are associated with faithful service and obedience to God, but they are not the basis for salvation itself.

3) Salvation Is by Grace: The belief that salvation is by grace alone is derived from passages such as Ephesians 2:8–9 NIV, which states, "For it is by grace you have been saved, through faith—and this is not from yourselves, it is the gift of God—not by works, so that no one can boast." This emphasizes that salvation is a free gift from God and cannot be earned through personal efforts or good deeds alone.

Reward Is by Good Works: (2 Cor. 5:10) It speaks about the future judgement and the rewards for our actions. "For we must all appear before the judgment seat of Christ, that each one may receive the things done in the body, according to what he has done, whether good or bad." This verse underscores the accountability of believers for their deeds and the anticipation of receiving awards or consequences based on their actions during their earthly life.

4) Salvation Is Obtained Instantly (John 6:47): It is through faith in Jesus Christ. Jesus says, "Most assuredly, I say to you, he who believes in Me has everlasting life." This emphasizes that by believing in Jesus, one receives the gift of eternal life and is saved from the penalty of sin. When a person trusts in Him as their Lord and Savior, they are justified before God and forgiven of their sins. This instant justification is the beginning of their salvation journey. The Bible states that believers are born again and receive the Holy Spirit as a guarantee of their future inheritance (John 3:3–7; Eph. 1:13–14).

Reward Will Be Obtained Later (Matt. 16:27): It states, "For the Son of Man will come in the glory of His Father with His angels, and then He will reward each according to his works." This verse suggests that when Jesus returns, there will be a judgment where individuals will be rewarded based on their actions and deeds. The rewards or blessings that accompany salvation are often described as being experienced in the future. The Bible speaks about the concept of rewards in several passages, particularly in relation to the final judgment and the eternal life to come (1 Cor. 3:12–15; Matt. 25:21; Rev. 22:12).

5) Salvation Is for the Unworthy (Luke 15:21): The passage describes the story of the prodigal son who returns to his father after squandering his inheritance. The son realizes his unworthiness and expresses repentance, saying, "And the son said to him, 'Father, I have sinned against heaven and in your sight, and am no longer worthy to be called your son.'" Despite feeling unworthy, the son seeks reconciliation with his father and is received with love and forgiveness.

Reward Is for the Worthy (1 Cor. 3:14): The verse speaks about rewards in the context of believers' works being tested by fire. It says, "If anyone's work which he has built on it endures, he will receive a reward." This passage emphasizes that there will be rewards for faithful service, and the quality of one's work in the service of God will be evaluated.

6) Salvation Cannot Be Lost (John 6:39 NIV): The verse states, "And this is the will of him who sent me, that I shall lose none of all those he has given me, but raise them up at the last day." This verse emphasizes the security of believers in Christ, suggesting that once someone has genuinely placed their faith in Jesus, they will be raised up on the last day and not be lost.

Reward Can Be Lost (1 Cor. 3:15 NIV): It discusses the idea of rewards and loss of rewards in the context of believers' works being tested by fire. It says, "If it is burned up, the builder will suffer loss but yet will be saved—even though only as one escaping through the flames." This verse implies that while a believer's works may be burned up and result in loss of rewards, they themselves will still be saved.

7) Salvation Guarantees Eternal Life (John 10:10 NIV): Jesus says, "The thief comes only to steal and kill and destroy; I have come that they may have life and have it to the full". This verse highlights the purpose of Jesus's coming to earth, which was not only to provide salvation and eternal life but also to offer abundant life to believers. Salvation, which is received through faith in Jesus Christ, assures believers of eternal life with God. It is the forgiveness of sins and the reconciliation with God that enables this eternal relationship.

Reward Is for Abundant Life (John 10:10): When Jesus speaks of "life to the full" or "abundant life," He is referring to a rich and meaningful life that encompasses more than just eternal existence. The abundant life involves experiencing a deep and intimate relationship with God, knowing His love and guidance, and living according to His principles and purposes. The abundant life Jesus offers doesn't guarantee a life free from challenges, suffering, or difficult circumstances. However, it does provide believers with the assurance that God is with them, guiding and strengthening them through those trials.

8) Salvation Is God's Part (John 19:30): Jesus says, "It is finished." This statement refers to Jesus's completed work on the cross, where He offered Himself as a sacrifice for the sins of humanity. It signifies the fulfillment of God's plan for salvation. In the context of salvation, it emphasizes that Jesus's sacrifice is the central aspect of God's work in bringing about redemption. Salvation is made possible through God's grace and the sacrificial death of Jesus Christ.

   Reward Is Man's Part (1 Cor. 9:24–27): It uses the analogy of a race to illustrate the perseverance and self-discipline required in the Christian life. The passage states that runners in a race all compete, but only one receives the prize. It encourages believers to run in such a way as to win the imperishable prize. The concept of rewards in the Christian life refers to the blessings, crowns, and eternal rewards that God promises to give to His faithful followers, not as a means of earning salvation but as a response to their obedience and faithfulness.

For a Christian, salvation is the foundational belief in Christianity that through faith in Jesus Christ, individuals are saved from the consequences of sin and reconciled with God. It is a free gift of grace, not earned through good works or personal merit. The reward, on the other hand, refers to the blessings and benefits that await believers in the afterlife. These rewards are described in various ways in the Bible, such as crowns, treasures in heaven, or positions of authority and responsibility. In essence, salvation is the starting point for a Christian's relationship with God, securing their eternal destiny in heaven. The reward, however, serves as an incentive for believers to live a life that honors God, following his teachings, and serving others. It motivates Christians to persevere in faith, pursue righteousness, and prioritize spiritual growth and the well-being of others.

PART TWO

COMPARE AND CONTRAST ASPECTS OF SALVATION

34. SALVATION AND GOOD WORKS

The relationship between salvation and good works can be understood within the framework of Christian theology. Two key passages in the Bible shed light on this relationship: Ephesians 2:8–10. Let's examine them one by one. These verses involve understanding the Christian concept of salvation and the role of good works in the life of a believer.

1. **Salvation** (Eph. 2:8–9 NIV): In Christian theology, salvation refers to the deliverance of a person from sin and its consequences, resulting in reconciliation with God and the promise of eternal life. This salvation is a free gift from God, made possible through faith in Jesus Christ. Ephesians 2:8–9 emphasizes the centrality of faith in salvation, stating, "For it is by grace you have been saved, through faith—and this is not from yourselves, it is the gift of God—not by works, so that no one can boast." This passage emphasizes that salvation is not earned through personal efforts or good works but is received as a gift of God's grace through faith alone. In other words, salvation is not something we achieve by our own actions or deeds but is a result of God's unmerited favor toward us. It is His grace that redeems us, lifting us from the depths of sin and offering us reconciliation with Him.

2. **Good Works** (Eph. 2:10 NIV): However, Ephesians 2:10 follows this statement by saying, "For we are God's handiwork, created in Christ Jesus to do good works, which God prepared in advance for us to do." This verse highlights that although good works do not contribute to

one's initial salvation, they are an essential outworking and evidence of genuine faith and salvation. In other words, while good works cannot save a person, they naturally flow from a heart transformed by God's grace. When someone genuinely receives salvation through faith, their life is transformed, and they begin to exhibit the fruit of the Spirit, including acts of kindness, love, compassion, and service to others. These good works are not performed to earn salvation or boast about personal achievements but rather as a response to the love and grace received from God. They become a natural expression of gratitude and a reflection of the new life in Christ. It is important to note that the emphasis on good works as evidence of salvation does not imply that salvation can be lost or earned through good works. The Bible consistently teaches that salvation is a gift received by faith in Jesus Christ. Good works, then, serve as a visible demonstration of one's faith and a reflection of the transforming power of God's grace.

Overall, the relationship between salvation and good works is that salvation is received through faith alone, but good works naturally follow as evidence of genuine faith and the transformed life that comes from being in a relationship with Christ. In summary, according to Christian theology, salvation is by grace through faith, apart from our works. However, genuine faith will produce good works as a natural outworking or evidence of that faith. Good works do not save us but rather indicate that our faith alive and genuine. They are the visible fruits of a transformed life, reflecting God's grace at work in us. Martin Luther had rightly said, "Good works cannot make a good man, but a good man makes good works." [22]

35. RELATIONSHIP AND FELLOWSHIP

As believers, our relationship with God is a profound and transformative experience that begins when we receive Jesus Christ as our Savior. This relationship is described in the Bible and is characterized by the forgiveness of sins and the restoration of our connection with God. Salvation is the initial step that brings believers into a new relationship with God, where they experience forgiveness and have permanent relationship with Him by His blood. However, believers are also called to continually confess their sins and seek forgiveness, acknowledging their ongoing need for God's grace

COMPARE AND CONTRAST ASPECTS OF SALVATION

and mercy. This ongoing fellowship with God is essential for a vibrant and growing Christian life.

Once-and-For-All Experience

1. **Relationship Is Salvation** (1 John 1:7b): Relationship with God begins at the moment of salvation and can never be broken. The phrase "the blood of Jesus Christ His Son cleanses us from all sin" emphasizes the central message of Christianity. According to Christian belief, humanity is inherently sinful and separated from God. However, through the sacrifice of Jesus Christ, who shed his blood on the cross, believers can be reconciled with God and receive salvation. The blood of Jesus is seen as a symbol of atonement, forgiveness, and cleansing from sin forever. This verse emphasizes the transformative power of salvation. When a person accepts Jesus Christ as their Lord and Savior, believing in his sacrificial death and resurrection, they enter a new relationship with God. They are forgiven of their sins and granted eternal life. This relationship is characterized by closeness and communion with God, with the believer being adopted as a child of God and becoming part of the family of believers.

   When we accept Jesus Christ as our Lord and Savior, we are reconciled to God and become His children. This relationship is not based on our own efforts or merits but on the grace and love of God. Through Jesus's sacrificial death and resurrection, we are forgiven and restored to a right standing with God. This relationship is eternal, meaning it lasts forever and cannot be broken or revoked. It is a personal connection with our heavenly Father, characterized by love, intimacy, and guidance. It brings us into the family of God, allowing us to experience His presence, peace, and eternal life.

Ongoing Experience

2. **Fellowship Is Christian Living** (1 John 1:8–10): Fellowship with God can be interrupted when we sin. Verse 8 states, "If we say that we have no sin, we deceive ourselves, and the truth is not in us." This verse acknowledges the reality that even after experiencing salvation, believers still have a sin nature and can struggle with sin. It cautions

against self-deception and emphasizes the need for humility and honesty about one's own shortcomings.

Verse 9 says, "If we confess our sins, He is faithful and just to forgive us our sins and to cleanse us from all unrighteousness." This verse encourages believers to confess their sins to God. Confession involves acknowledging and admitting one's sins before God, seeking His forgiveness, and turning away from those sins. It assures believers that God is faithful and just to forgive them when they confess, and that He will cleanse them from all unrighteousness. This ongoing process of confession and forgiveness helps maintain the fellowship between believers and God.

Verse 10 further emphasizes the universal nature of human sinfulness, stating, "If we say that we have not sinned, we make Him a liar, and His word is not in us." It reinforces the idea that no one is exempt from sin and that claiming to be without sin is to reject the truth of God's Word.

While our relationship with God is eternal and unchanging, our fellowship with Him can fluctuate over time. Fellowship refers to our active communion, intimacy, and interaction with God in our daily lives. It is a dynamic aspect of our relationship with Him. Our relationship with God is established when we accept Jesus Christ as our Savior, and it is an eternal bond characterized by love, forgiveness, and divine adoption. On the other hand, our fellowship with God is the ongoing, day-to-day communion and intimacy we experience with Him, which can be affected by our choices and actions. By actively pursuing a vibrant fellowship with God through obedience, confession, and repentance, we can enjoy the fullness of His presence and experience the joy and blessings that come from walking in close communion with our heavenly Father.

36. POSITION AND PRACTICE

In Christian theology, righteousness is often divided into two distinct aspects: positional righteousness and practical righteousness. These two components play a crucial role in understanding the relationship between faith and works within the context of salvation. While positional righteousness is the foundation of the Christian's relationship with God, practical righteousness is the outworking and expression of that relationship in daily life. It is a response to God's grace and a manifestation of genuine faith. The pursuit of practical righteousness is not a means to earn salvation but rather a natural outcome of being transformed by God's love and grace.

1. **Positional Righteousness "Justification"** (Rom. 3:24)

    1) Definition: Positional righteousness refers to the act of God declaring a person righteous by faith in Jesus Christ, based on His atoning work on the cross. It is a legal or forensic declaration that occurs at the moment of salvation.

    2) Basis: Positional righteousness is solely based on the finished work of Christ. It is not earned or achieved by human efforts or good works.

    3) Source: It comes from the grace of God through faith in Jesus Christ (Eph. 2:8–9). It is a gift from God and is received through belief in Christ's sacrificial death and resurrection.

    4) Instantaneous: Positional righteousness is received the moment a person places their faith in Jesus Christ. It is a one-time event that permanently changes the believer's standing before God.

    5) Eternal and Unchanging: It is grounded in the finished work of Christ on the cross. It means that once a person is justified by faith in Christ, they are declared righteous in the sight of God.

    6) Imputed Righteousness: The righteousness of Christ is imputed or credited to the believer. The believer's sins are forgiven, and they are seen as righteous in God's sight.

    7) External Change: It is an objective declaration made by God concerning the believer's legal standing before Him. It does not inherently change the person's internal nature or character. Instead, it provides a foundation for the believer's relationship with God, reconciling them to Him and removing the guilt and penalty of sin.

2. **Practical Righteousness "Sanctification"** (1 Thess. 5:23)

   1) Definition: Practical righteousness, also known as sanctification, refers to the ongoing process of being conformed to the likeness of Christ in character and conduct. It is the daily transformation of a believer's life to live in accordance with God's will.

   2) Cooperation: Sanctification involves the cooperation of the believer with the work of the Holy Spirit. While justification is an act of God alone, sanctification requires the active participation of the believer.

   3) Progressive: Sanctification is a lifelong process that continues throughout the believer's life. It involves growth, maturity, and spiritual development as the believer is empowered by the Holy Spirit to live a life of obedience to God's commands.

   4) Transformation: Sanctification involves the renewal of the mind and heart, leading to a change in behavior and character. It includes the process of overcoming sinful habits, developing virtues, and aligning one's life with biblical principles.

   5) Temporal Change: It is a lifelong journey characterized by growth, maturity, and the process of being conformed to the likeness of Christ. Through the indwelling presence of the Holy Spirit.

   6) Evidential: Practical righteousness produces tangible fruits in the life of a believer, such as love, joy, peace, patience, kindness, goodness, faithfulness, gentleness, and self-control (Gal. 5:22–23). These qualities reflect the inward transformation occurring through the process of sanctification.

   7) Internal Change: It refers to the ongoing process of internal change and transformation that occurs in the life of a believer after justification. It is the work of the Holy Spirit within the believer, enabling them to grow in holiness, conforming them more and more to the image of Christ.

While positional righteousness (justification) and practical righteousness (sanctification) are essential aspects of the Christian faith, they differ in their nature, basis, timing, and ongoing process. Positional righteousness establishes the believer's standing before God based on faith in Christ, while practical righteousness involves the daily transformation and growth of the believer's character and conduct. They are integral aspects of the Christian faith, emphasizing the inseparable relationship between faith and works in the life of a believer.

37. LAW AND GRACE

The Christian doctrine of law and grace stands at the heart of Christian theology, representing a profound tension between the demands of divine law and the unmerited gift of God's grace. This doctrine is central to understanding the relationship between humanity and God, and it shapes the Christian understanding of salvation and the nature of the Christian life. Throughout history, theologians and believers alike have grappled with the complexities of balancing God's moral requirements, as expressed in the law of the Old Testament, with the radical concept of grace introduced by Jesus Christ in the New Testament (John 1:16–17).

1. **Law:** The law was given by God to the people of Israel through Moses in the Old Testament. It was to guide the Israelites in their worship of God, establish a moral and ethical framework, and set the nation of Israel apart as God's chosen people. The law is divided into three categories: the ceremonial laws, the civil laws, and the moral laws. The purpose of the law is to communicate God's holy and perfect standard for righteous living. Another purpose of the law is to define sin and reveal man's sinful nature and the extent to which humanity falls short of God's perfect standard of righteousness. The law reveals to us the consequences of living in sin or in rebellion against God. The law cannot save a sinner, but the final purpose of the law is to lead us to the foot of the cross, to Jesus Christ. (Rom. 3:19–20; Gal. 3:23–25).

2. **Grace:** Grace, on the other hand, is an expression of God's unmerited favor and love toward humanity. It is often associated with the new covenant brought by Jesus Christ. Grace emphasizes that salvation

and reconciliation with God are not earned through human efforts or adherence to the law but are freely given by God through faith in Jesus Christ. No one can perfectly fulfill the requirements of the law due to human imperfection and sin. This is where the concept of grace comes into play. Grace is the undeserved favor that God extends to humanity. We are justified by grace as a gift through the redemption that is Christ Jesus. However, grace does not give people a license to sin or disobey God's moral laws. Our understanding of the true grace of God's will lead us to a life of godliness instead of lawlessness. When we receive God's grace and what Christ did for us on the cross by giving His life for sinners, we will respond by wanting to live a godly life (Eph. 2:8–9; Rom. 3:23–26; Gal. 5:13; Jude 1:4).

The contrast between law and grace does not mean that the law is irrelevant or abolished but rather that it has been fulfilled in Christ (Matt. 5:17; Rom. 10:4). Believers are no longer under the law as a means of justification but are guided by the principles of love and righteousness, empowered by the grace of God. Overall, the law highlights humanity's need for a Savior, while grace reveals God's mercy and provision through Jesus Christ, offering forgiveness, redemption, and the empowerment to live a transformed life.

COMPARE AND CONTRAST ASPECTS OF SALVATION

The Difference between Law and Grace

Law	Grace
1. Through Moses at Sinai (John 1:17)	1. Through Christ at Calvary
2. On tablets of stone (2 Cor. 3:3)	2. On tablets of flesh
3. Not sufficient (2 Cor. 3:5)	3. Sufficient
4. The letter kills (2 Cor. 3:6)	4. The Spirit gives life
5. Ministry of death (2 Cor. 3:7)	5. Ministry of life
6. Condemnation (2 Cor. 3:9)	6. Ministry of righteousness
7. No glory (2 Cor. 3:10)	7. Glory
8. Veiled (2 Cor. 3:14)	8. Unveiled
9. No liberty (2 Cor. 3:17)	9. Liberty
10. Condemn the best (Jas. 2:10)	10. Justify the worst (1 Tim. 1:15)
11. Should be stoned (John 8:5)	11. Jesus does not condemn (John 8:11)
12. Reveal sin (Rom. 3:20)	12. Reveal salvation (Rom. 10:2)
13. Curse the law keeper (Gal. 3:10–12)	13. Redeem the cursed (Gal. 3:13)
14. Something to boast (Rom. 4:1–2)	14. Nothing to boast (Rom. 4:3–5)
15. Command and demand (Col. 2:21)	15. Provide and protect (John 6:39)
16. No repentance (Luke 18:9–14)	16. Genuine repentance
17. Old covenant (Heb. 8:10)	17. New covenant
18. Remember sins (Heb. 8:12)	18. Remember sins no more
19. Vanish away (Heb. 8:13)	19. Make it obsolete
20. Bring us to Christ (Gal. 3:24)	20. No longer under law (Gal. 3:25)
21. Confined all under sin (Gal. 3:22)	21. Freedom to believers
22. Hagar, bondwoman (Gal. 4:22)	22. Sarah, free woman
23. Natural water (John 4:13)	23. Supernatural water (John 4:14)
24. Sin is hidden (John 4:17)	24. Sin is exposed (John 4:39)
25. Hate your enemy (Matt. 5:43)	25. Love your enemy (Matt. 5:44)
26. Justice (Rom. 5:16a)	26. Grace (Rom. 5:16b)
27. Do it for salvation (Gal. 3:10)	27. It is done for salvation (John 19:30)
28. Trying for salvation (Rom. 3:28)	28. Trusting for salvation
29. Imperfection (Heb. 10:1)	29. Perfection (Heb. 10:14)
30. Demand holiness (1 Pet. 1:16)	30. Provide holiness (Heb. 10:10)
31. Demand perfection (Matt. 5:48)	31. Provide perfection (Heb. 10:14)
32. Have to do things for God's love	32. Get to do things for God's love
33. The wages of sin is death (Rom. 6:23)	33. The gift of God is eternal life
34. Lost in Adam, all die (1 Cor. 15:22)	34. Saved in Christ, all live
35. Works of the flesh (Gal. 5:19–21)	35. Fruit of the Spirit (Gal. 5:22–23)
36. Do and live (Deut. 8:1)	36. Live and do
37. Every mouth stop (Rom. 3:19)	37. Confess with mouth (Rom. 10:9)

38. Favor to the good (Prov. 12:2)	38. Favor the ungodly (Eph. 2:1–6)
39. It retaliates (Exod. 21:24)	39. It redeems (Gal. 3:13)
40. 3000 were slain (Exod. 32:28)	40. 3000 were saved (Acts 2:41)
41. Yoke is heavy (Gal. 5:1)	41. Yoke is easy (Matt. 11:29–30)
42. The soul that sin shall die (Ezek. 18:4)	42. The one who believes shall live
43. Man must do for God	43. Christ has done for man
44. Death (Rom. 5:14)	44. Life
45. One Offense "Condemned" (Rom. 5:16)	45. Many offenses "justified"
46. Condemnation (Rom. 5:18)	46. Justification
47. Disobedience (Rom. 5:19)	47. Obedience
48. Continual sacrifices (Heb. 10:11)	48. Once-for-all sacrifice (Heb. 10:12)
49. Old creation (2 Cor. 5:17)	49. New creation
50. A slave of sin (John 8:34)	50. The Son makes you free (John 8:36)

As Christians navigate the complexities of their faith, they are invited to embrace the moral guidance found in the law and the liberating grace offered through Christ. This harmony between law and grace shapes not only their relationship with God but also their interactions with fellow humans, inspiring compassion, forgiveness, and the pursuit of justice. Ultimately, the doctrine of law and grace encourages believers to approach their spiritual journey with humility, recognizing their dependence on God's grace while striving to honor the principles of righteousness.

38. GRACE AND MERCY

Grace and mercy are two fundamental aspects of the Christian faith that hold immense significance for believers. In Christian theology, grace and mercy are closely intertwined, representing the unconditional love and forgiveness bestowed upon humanity through the redemptive work of Jesus Christ. Philip Wijaya writes in his 2023 work, "Grace means getting what we do not deserve, namely heaven, and Mercy means not getting what we deserve, namely hell" (Wijaya 2023).[23]

1. **Grace** (Eph. 2:8–9): Grace refers to the unmerited favor and love of God extended toward humanity. It is the unearned and undeserved kindness and goodwill of God. In these verses, the apostle Paul emphasizes that salvation and forgiveness of sins are not achieved through our own efforts, good works, or personal merit. Instead, they are freely

COMPARE AND CONTRAST ASPECTS OF SALVATION

given by God through His grace. This means that salvation is a gift from God that cannot be earned but is received by faith. It is an act of God's grace that offers forgiveness and eternal life to all who believe in Jesus Christ. In other words, salvation is not something we can earn or achieve through our own efforts; it is a gift freely given by God through His grace.

Through grace, God offers forgiveness and reconciliation to all who believe in Him. Despite our flaws, shortcomings, and sins, God extends His grace to us, inviting us into a relationship with Him. It is through this grace that we experience the transformative power of Christ's sacrifice on the cross, as His death and resurrection provide the means for our salvation. By accepting God's grace, we are set free from the bondage of sin and receive the promise of eternal life with Him.

2. **Mercy (Eph. 2:4):** Mercy refers to God's compassion and withholding of the punishment that humanity deserves due to sin. It involves God's tenderheartedness and His decision to not give us the judgment we deserve. In this verse, Paul highlights God's mercy by stating that even though we were spiritually dead because of our sins, God, out of His great love, mercy, and compassion, made us alive in Christ. This mercy is expressed through God's willingness to forgive and restore us to a right relationship with Him, even though we have sinned against Him.

Mercy, on the other hand, complements the concept of grace. While grace refers to God's unmerited favor, mercy encompasses His compassion and forbearance toward those who have fallen short of His perfect standards. The Bible reminds us that "the wages of sin is death" (Rom. 6:23a), highlighting the reality of sin's consequences. However, God's mercy intervenes, offering us an alternative outcome. Instead of receiving the punishment we deserve, God, in His mercy, extends forgiveness and withholds the judgment we have earned. Through the life and ministry of Jesus Christ, we witness the embodiment of God's mercy. Jesus continually reached out to the marginalized, the outcasts, and the sinners of society, demonstrating God's compassionate nature and His desire to reconcile humanity to Himself. The ultimate act of mercy was displayed on the cross when Jesus willingly took upon

Himself the sins of the world, offering salvation to all who would believe in Him.

Grace and mercy in Christ are central to the Christian faith. Through God's grace, we are offered salvation and a restored relationship with Him, not based on our own merits but on His unmerited favor. His mercy brings forgiveness and compassion, providing an opportunity for reconciliation and healing. As recipients of God's grace and mercy, we are called to extend these gifts to others, reflecting the love of Christ in our interactions and embodying His transformative power in the world. Both concepts reveal God's love, kindness, and willingness to offer salvation and new life to humanity through faith in Jesus Christ.

39. TWO GARMENTS

The concept of "The Garment of Salvation" and the comparison between "The Garment of Adam" and "The Garment of Jesus Christ" appears to be related to biblical interpretations and symbolism. Let's break down each part:

1. **The Garment of Adam** (Gen. 3:7 NIV; Isa. 64:6 NIV): In the book of Genesis, specifically in Genesis 3:7, after Adam and Eve ate the forbidden fruit from the Tree of Knowledge of Good and Evil, their eyes were opened, and they realized they were naked. Feeling ashamed and exposed, they sewed fig leaves together to make themselves loincloths as a means to cover their nakedness. Genesis 3:7 says: "Then the eyes of both of them were opened, and they realized they were naked; so they sewed fig leaves together and made coverings for themselves." This event represents the introduction of sin and the fall of humankind, as they disobeyed God's command and lost their innocence. The fig leaves, though an attempt to cover themselves, they were inadequate as mere human efforts could not truly restore their righteousness or address the root of their sinfulness. Isaiah 64:6 emphasizes the insufficiency of human righteousness in the eyes of God: "All of us have become like one who is unclean, and all our righteous acts are like filthy rags; we all shrivel up like a leaf, and like the wind, our sins sweep us away." The

analogy of "filthy rags" conveys that human efforts to attain salvation or cover their sins are ineffective and insufficient in the eyes of God.

2. **The Garment of Jesus Christ** (Gen. 3:21 NIV; Gal. 3:26–27 NIV): In contrast to the inadequate fig leaves, the Bible also presents the concept of God providing proper clothes to cover the shame of humanity. This is seen symbolically in Genesis 3:21, where, after pronouncing curses due to their sin, God makes garments of skin to clothe Adam and Eve. Genesis 3:21 says: "The Lord God made garments of skin for Adam and his wife and clothed them." This act foreshadows the need for a proper and lasting solution to cover humanity's sinfulness. The garments of skin imply the first animal sacrifice, prefiguring the ultimate sacrifice of Jesus Christ, who would provide a way for humanity's sins to be covered and forgiven. In the New Testament, specifically in Galatians 3:26–27 NIV, the clothing analogy takes on a deeper spiritual meaning. It speaks of being clothed with Christ through faith and baptism, representing a transformation and identification with Jesus, where believers put on His righteousness. Galatians 3:26–27 says: "So in Christ Jesus, you are all children of God through faith, for all of you who were baptized into Christ have clothed yourselves with Christ." In this sense, believers, through their faith in Jesus Christ, become righteous in God's sight, not by their own efforts but by being clothed with the righteousness of Christ.

The transition from fig leaves to garments of skin symbolizes the shift from human attempts to cover shame to God's provision for redemption. The fig leaves represent inadequate human efforts, while the garments of skin, provided by God, signify divine grace and sacrifice. This early biblical narrative foreshadows the need for a sacrificial atonement and points towards the overarching theme of God's redemptive plan throughout Scripture.

40. TWO GRACE

The concept of grace refers to the unmerited favor or gift of God extended to humanity. It is an essential aspect of the Christian faith and is described in various ways in the Bible. Two kinds of grace often discussed are common grace and special or saving grace.

1. **Common Grace:** It is also known as general grace or universal grace, refers to the gracious actions of God toward all of creation, regardless of their spiritual state or relationship with God. It is called "common" because it is extended to all people in a general sense, without regard to their specific faith or belief. Matthew 5:45 NIV alludes to this concept when Jesus says, "He causes his sun to rise on the evil and the good, and sends rain on the righteous and the unrighteous." Common grace encompasses various blessings and provisions that God bestows upon humanity as a whole. These include the natural order and laws that sustain the universe, intellectual capacities, moral conscience, artistic talents, and societal structures. Through common grace, God demonstrates his goodness and care for all people, whether they acknowledge him or not. It is a way in which God expresses his love and mercy to the entire creation.

2. **Special or Saving Grace:** It is the specific and extraordinary grace of God that brings about salvation and redemption. It is distinct from common grace in that it is not universally applied but is extended to those who respond to God's call in faith. Romans 11:6 NIV touches on this kind of grace, stating, "And if by grace, then it cannot be based on works; if it were, grace would no longer be grace." Special grace is often associated with the work of Jesus Christ and his sacrifice on the cross. It is through this grace that God offers forgiveness, reconciliation, and eternal life to humanity. It is not something that can be earned or achieved through human effort or merit but is received through faith in Jesus Christ. Special grace is transformative, as it not only forgives sins but also empowers believers to live in accordance with God's will and purposes.

In summary, common grace encompasses the general blessings and provisions that God extends to all of creation, while special or saving grace is the specific grace of God that brings about salvation and eternal life through faith in Jesus Christ. Both types of grace reveal God's goodness, love, and mercy, albeit in different ways and to different extents.

41. TWO BIRTHS

In the profound verses of John 3:3–5, we encounter a remarkable duality that encapsulates the essence of human existence and spiritual transformation. This passage delves into the concept of two births—the first birth, born of flesh, and the second birth, born of the Spirit. Within these verses, the deeper meanings of life's journey and the transformative power of spirituality are unveiled. Let us explore the significance of these two births and their implications on the human experience.

1. **First Birth, Born of Flesh:** The first birth, born of flesh, represents our physical entry into this world. It marks the moment when we are brought forth from the womb, becoming part of the tangible and material realm. This birth signifies our connection to the temporal and earthly aspects of existence. Through this birth, we are introduced to the intricate tapestry of life, filled with experiences, emotions, and relationships. It is a birth that binds us to the limitations of the physical realm, subjecting us to the transient nature of the material world.

2. **Second Birth, Born of the Spirit:** In contrast, the second birth, born of the Spirit, delves into the realm of the intangible and divine. This birth represents a spiritual awakening, a rebirth of the soul that transcends the confines of the flesh. It signifies a profound transformation brought about by the influence of the Holy Spirit. Through this birth, we undergo a metamorphosis of the heart and mind, embracing a deeper understanding of our spiritual purpose and connection to the eternal. It is a birth that liberates us from the limitations of the physical and grants us entry into the realm of spiritual enlightenment and communion with the divine.

Key Differences between the First and Second Birth

1) Nature: The first birth is physical and natural, while the second birth is spiritual and supernatural.

2) Origin: The first birth originates from human parents, while the second birth originates from God through the work of the Holy Spirit.

3) Condition: The first birth leaves a person in a state of spiritual separation from God due to inherited sin, while the second birth reconciles the person to God, bringing about spiritual renewal and restoration.

4) Purpose: The first birth enables a person to live and function in the physical world, while the second birth brings about spiritual transformation, leading to a new purpose in life centered on serving God and living according to His will.

5) Outcome: The first birth leads to physical life on earth, which is temporary and subject to death, while the second birth leads to eternal life and the hope of salvation in the presence of God.

The dichotomy of the two births presented in John 3:3–5 encapsulates the intricate dance between the material and the spiritual, the finite and the infinite. The first birth, born of flesh, initiates our earthly journey, while the second birth, born of the Spirit, heralds a transformative awakening to the spiritual dimensions of existence. Together, these births weave a tapestry of human experience, inviting us to navigate the complex interplay between the tangible and the transcendent. As we reflect on this profound teaching, may we embrace the call to embark on a journey of spiritual rebirth, allowing the winds of the Spirit to guide us toward a deeper understanding of our true identity and purpose.

42. TWO DEMANDS

According to Christian theology, humans are considered to be inherently sinful and unable to meet God's standard of holiness and perfection on their own. Despite our best efforts, we are prone to sin and are unable to achieve the level of holiness and perfection that God requires. This separation from God's holiness is often referred to as "sin," which is the disobedience or missing the mark of God's perfect standard. The Bible emphasizes the insufficiency of human efforts to achieve salvation and stresses the significance of Jesus Christ's sacrifice.

COMPARE AND CONTRAST ASPECTS OF SALVATION

1. **God Demands Holiness** (1 Pet. 1:15–16)

   1) Holiness is Demanded: The Bible, specifically in 1 Peter 1:15–16 NIV, states, "But just as he who called you is holy, so be holy in all you do; for it is written: 'Be holy, because I am holy.'" This passage emphasizes the expectation for believers to strive for holiness in their thoughts, actions, and character, reflecting the nature of God.

   2) Man's Failure (Job 15:14): It highlights the inherent imperfection of humanity before a holy God. It states, "What is man, that he could be pure? And he who is born of a woman, that he could be righteous?" This verse acknowledges the fallen state of humanity and its inability to attain perfect holiness on its own. Throughout the Bible, there is a recognition that all human beings fall short of God's perfect standard of holiness (Rom. 3:23).

   3) God's Solution (Heb. 10:10 NIV): It states, "And by that will, we have been made holy through the sacrifce of the body of Jesus Christ once for all." This verse highlights the idea that Jesus's sacrifice on the cross was a definitive and sufficient act to make believers holy in the eyes of God. It suggests that through Jesus's sacrifice, believers can be reconciled with God and receive forgiveness for their sins.

2. **God Demands Perfection** (Matt. 5:48)

   1) Perfection Is Demanded: God said, "Therefore you shall be perfect, just as your Father in heaven is perfect," emphasizing the high moral standard set by God. This verse reflects the ideal of moral perfection that humans are called to strive for.

   2) Man's Failure (Heb.10:1): It speaks more broadly about the limitations of the Old Testament sacrificial system in providing permanent forgiveness of sins. It points to the need for a perfect and ultimate sacrifice to cleanse humanity from sin, which is fulfilled in the person of Jesus Christ.

3) God's Solution (Hebrews 10:14 NIV): "For by one sacrifice he has made perfect forever those who are being made holy." This verse expresses the belief that through Jesus's sacrifice, believers are made perfect, and their sins are forgiven once and for all. It acknowledges that the process of sanctification, or becoming holy, is ongoing, but the foundation for this transformation is established through the sacrifice of Jesus Christ.

In summary, while God does demand holiness and perfection, it is acknowledged that human beings, due to their fallen nature, are incapable of achieving it on their own. It is recognized that human beings are inherently flawed and prone to sin as a result of the fall of humanity in the garden of Eden. This inherited sin nature separates humanity from God and makes it impossible for individuals to achieve holiness and perfection on their own. It is only through faith in Jesus Christ and his sacrificial death on the cross that individuals can find forgiveness for their sins and be reconciled with God. It is through this relationship with God and the empowering presence of the Holy Spirit that Christians can strive to live in accordance with God's perfect will, even though they may still fall short at times.

43. TWO FORGIVENESS

In John 13:4–11, Jesus is demonstrating humility and service by washing the feet of his disciples. However, his actions hold a deeper meaning beyond the physical act of washing feet. Jesus uses this metaphor to illustrate the concepts of eternal forgiveness and temporal forgiveness. So, Jesus uses the metaphor of bathing to represent the initial, eternal forgiveness we receive through faith and the metaphor of foot washing to represent the ongoing, temporal forgiveness we need in our daily lives. Both aspects are essential for believers to experience the fullness of God's forgiveness and maintain a close relationship with Him.

1. **Eternal Forgiveness** (Taking a Bath): In Christianity, the idea of eternal forgiveness refers to the forgiveness of sins granted by God through faith in Jesus Christ. This forgiveness is everlasting and granted to individuals who repent and place their trust in Jesus as their Savior. The metaphor of taking a bath is often used to symbolize the cleansing

of sin through God's forgiveness. By acknowledging their sins, asking for forgiveness, and accepting Jesus as their Savior, believers believe they are spiritually cleansed and receive eternal forgiveness. The metaphor of bathing represents eternal forgiveness. Jesus tells Peter that those who have had a bath (those who have accepted him and received his forgiveness) are already clean. This refers to the initial forgiveness that comes through faith in Jesus and his sacrifice on the cross. It is a once-for-all forgiveness that washes away all our sins, past, present, and future, and reconciles us with God for eternity. It is a spiritual cleansing that makes us completely clean before God (1 John 1:7b). Jesus explained that when a sinner trusts the Savior he is 'bathed all over' as his sins are washed away and forgiven. However, as the believer walks in the world, it is easy to become defiled. He does not need to be bathed again but simply needs to have that defilement cleansed (1 John 1:9) as mentioned below.

2. **Temporal Forgiveness** (Foot Washing): On the other hand, the metaphor of foot washing represents temporal forgiveness. In this passage, Jesus performs the act of washing his disciples' feet as a symbolic gesture of humility and service. Peter, one of the disciples, initially refuses to let Jesus. Jesus explains to Peter that even though he is already clean, he still needs his feet to be washed. Peter then asks Jesus to wash not only his feet but also his hands and head. Jesus responds by saying that those who have bathed only need to have their feet washed and are clean. The act of foot washing in this context is seen as a metaphor for Jesus's forgiveness and cleansing of believers from their personal sins. It represents the ongoing need for believers to seek forgiveness for their daily shortcomings and sins. While they may have already received eternal forgiveness through faith in Jesus, they still require temporal forgiveness to maintain a close relationship with God and live a life of purity and righteousness. This refers to the ongoing process of forgiveness that believers experience in their daily lives. Our feet symbolize our walk, our actions, and the ways we may stumble and sin along the way. Through foot washing, Jesus teaches that we need continual forgiveness and cleansing as we journey through life. This forgiveness is available to us as we confess our sins and seek God's forgiveness on a regular basis (1 John 1:8–10).

Here, we encounter a profound narrative that illuminates the transformative power of forgiveness. Eternal forgiveness, rooted in Jesus's redemptive work, offers reconciliation with God and eternal salvation. Simultaneously, temporal forgiveness, demonstrated through acts of humility and servanthood, facilitates healing, reconciliation, and restoration within our human relationships. By embracing eternal and temporal forgiveness, we align ourselves with God's character, cultivate compassion, and experience profound liberation and wholeness. May we be inspired by the example set forth by Jesus, and may the pursuit of forgiveness permeate our lives, fostering unity, love, and peace in our communities.

44. TWO RELATIONSHIPS

Understanding the importance of these two relationships requires a broader understanding of the message of salvation. The importance of these relationships lies in their contrasting outcomes. In Adam, all are subject to sin and death, but in Christ, by accepting Christ's sacrifice and developing a personal relationship with Him allows individuals to be born again spiritually, becoming partakers of God's divine nature and recipients of His grace. For Christians, the relationship with Adam represents their fallen state and the need for salvation, while the relationship with Christ signifies their redemption and hope of eternal life. It emphasizes the centrality of Christ's work on the cross and the necessity of faith in Him for salvation. The only solution to our problem of sin is to "change our parentage" (1 Cor. 15:22).

1. **Relationship with Adam:** Adam, as the first man, represents humanity's shared origin. Through his disobedience in the garden of Eden, sin entered the world, and its consequences—spiritual separation from God and death—were passed on to all of Adam's descendants. Adam's disobedience led to the introduction of a broken relationship between humanity and God. This broken relationship is often referred to as the "fall" and is a central tenet in Christian theology. This inherited sinful nature affects every individual, and apart from God's intervention, it leads to spiritual death and eternal hell. As through the sin of the first Adam, all men became mortal because all had from him the same sinful nature. When he disobeyed, he was disobeying on our behalf. All those born after him were born spiritually "dead on arrival" on earth. If we

remain only represented by Adam, there is no hope for us whatsoever (Rom. 5:12; 11:32).

2. **Relationship with Christ:** Jesus Christ, the Son of God, came to earth as the perfect and sinless sacrifice for humanity's sins. Through His death and resurrection, He conquered sin, overcame death, and provided a way for people to be reconciled with God. He came here for us. He came here on a mission to save His people from their sin (Matt. 1:21), and His mission was accomplished on the cross. Only because of Jesus Christ, humanity can be reconciled with God and its broken relationship restored. Jesus is often referred to as the "Second Adam" because, through his obedience and sacrifice, he offers redemption and the opportunity for a renewed relationship with God. Believers are considered to be "in Christ," meaning that they share in his righteousness and are united with him in a spiritual sense. By placing their faith in Christ and accepting His sacrifice, individuals can experience forgiveness, restoration, and eternal life. This relationship is once-for-all (John 19:30; Col. 1:20–21).

Compare and Contrast the Relationship with Adam and Christ

In Romans 5:14–20, Paul masterfully presents a stark contrast between Adam and Christ, highlighting the devastating impact of sin and the glorious redemption and restoration brought about by Christ's obedience. This passage underscores the centrality of Christ's work in overcoming sin and offers hope and assurance to all who believe in Him.

1. **Death and Life** (Rom. 5:14): "Nevertheless death reigned from Adam to Moses, even over those who had not sinned according to the likeness of the transgression of Adam, who is a type of Him who was to come." In this verse, Paul establishes Adam as a representative figure who brought sin and death into the world through his transgression. Adam's sin had universal consequences, leading to the reign of death over humanity. However, Paul also points out that Adam serves as a type, or foreshadowing, of Christ, who was to come as the ultimate solution for sin and its consequences.

2. **One Offense and Many Offenses** (Rom. 5:16): "And the gift is not like that which came through the one who sinned. For the judgment which came from one offense resulted in condemnation, but the free gift which came from many offenses resulted in justification." Here, Paul contrasts the effects of Adam's sin with the free gift of grace through Christ. Adam's sin led to condemnation for all humanity, whereas Christ's gift of grace provides justification and reconciliation with God. While the impact of Adam's sin was limited to one offense, Christ's gift covers many offenses, highlighting the abundance of God's grace.

3. **Condemnation and Justification** (Rom. 5:18): "Therefore, as through one man's offense judgment came to all men, resulting in condemnation, even so through one Man's righteous act the free gift came to all men, resulting in justification of life." Once again, Paul emphasizes the parallel between Adam and Christ. Through Adam's offense, all humanity experienced judgment and condemnation. However, through Christ's righteous act (referring to His death on the cross and subsequent resurrection), the free gift of justification and life is made available to all people. The impact of Christ's act is far-reaching, counteracting the consequences of Adam's sin.

4. **Disobedience and Obedience** (Rom. 5:19): "For as by one man's disobedience many were made sinners, so also by one Man's obedience many will be made righteous." Paul draws a comparison between Adam's disobedience and Christ's obedience. Through Adam's disobedience, many were made sinners, meaning that all humanity inherited a sinful nature. Conversely, through Christ's obedience, many will be made righteous. This righteousness is imputed to believers through faith in Christ, enabling them to stand before God as justified and righteous individuals.

5. **Law and Grace** (Rom. 5:20): "Moreover, the law entered that the offense might abound. But where sin abounded, grace abounded much more." In this verse, Paul mentions the role of the law in relation to sin and grace. The law was given to Israel through Moses, highlighting the offense of sin and making people aware of their transgressions. However, Paul emphasizes that where sin abounded, grace abounded even more. The grace of God, manifested through Christ, is greater

than the power of sin, providing a solution that surpasses the condemnation brought by the law.

Overall, these passages in Romans highlight the stark contrast between Adam and Christ. Adam's sin brought judgment, condemnation, and death to all humanity, while Christ's righteousness and obedience offer justification, reconciliation, and eternal life to those who believe in Him. Through Christ, God's grace and forgiveness far exceed the consequences of sin, demonstrating His redemptive plan for humanity.

45. TWO SONS

The parable focuses on themes of forgiveness, reconciliation, and the nature of God's love. It contrasts the repentance and humility of the younger son with the self-righteousness and lack of mercy displayed by the elder son. Both sons reveal different aspects of human nature and provide a backdrop for Jesus's teaching about God's unconditional love and the nature of redemption.

1. **Younger Son**: Prodigal Son: (Luke 15:11–24): This son represents tax collectors and sinners. He is characterized by his recklessness and sinful behavior. He asks for his share of the inheritance from his father and goes to a distant country, where he squanders his wealth on extravagant and sinful living. Eventually, he finds himself in a desperate situation, feeding pigs and longing to eat their food. This low point makes him realize the gravity of his actions and the depth of his unworthiness. He decides to return to his father, confess his sins, and ask for forgiveness. The father, in an act of profound mercy and love, welcomes him back with open arms, throwing a feast to celebrate his return.

2. **Elder Son**: Self-righteous Son: (Luke 15:25–32): This son represents the Pharisees and scribes, who were known for their self-righteousness and legalistic attitudes. When the younger son returns and the father throws a feast, the elder son becomes angry and refuses to join the celebration. He feels that he has always been obedient and deserving of his father's favor. His self-righteousness blinds him to the significance of his brother's return and his father's forgiveness. The father gently reminds him of the importance of compassion and forgiveness,

emphasizing that they should celebrate the younger son's return, as he was lost and is now found. The elder son's attitude reveals the danger of self-righteousness and pride, as he fails to grasp the essence of his father's love and mercy.

Jesus's ministry was characterized by his willingness to embrace and save sinners, regardless of their social status or reputation. He rejected the self-righteousness of the religious elite, emphasizing the importance of recognizing our own need for spiritual healing and forgiveness. This message remains relevant today, reminding us of the boundless grace and love that Jesus offers to all who come to him in humility and repentance.

46. TWO GATES

The broad gate and narrow gate represent two contrasting paths that individuals can choose in life. The broad gate symbolizes the easy, popular, and seemingly attractive route that the majority of people tend to follow. However, this path ultimately leads to destruction and spiritual emptiness. On the other hand, the narrow gate represents the less-traveled and more challenging path. It involves making difficult choices that lead to eternal life and true fulfillment in the presence of God.

1. **The Broad Gate** (Matt. 7:13)

    1) Destination: This is the path that leads to destruction and hell.

    2) Many who go in by it: Due to Adam's sin, the whole world is already on this path, and all are born spiritually dead in trespasses. People must decide whether to remain here or to flee. However, the majority tend to stay undecided. It is crucial to get off this path. The world system is spacious and easy to follow.

    3) It is easy: The broad gate represents man's system, focused on outward appearances and popularity. It is tempting and preferred by those who rely on self-righteousness, choosing good works over receiving the good news. The broad gate is the path of going with the flow and following the crowd, taking the path of least resistance. Many non-Christian religions, including nominal Christians,

pursue this gate through good works, finding it easier to rely on their own merits rather than receiving the gift of salvation offered through Christ.

2. **The Narrow Gate** (Matt. 7:14)

   1) Destination: This is the path that leads to life and heaven.

   2) There are few who find it: Only a few are chosen. The narrow gate is not attractive and popular. The gospel is veiled and blinded by the god of this age (2 Cor. 4:3–4).

   3) It is difficult: The narrow gate represents a divine plan involving inward change. Many in the world's population do not have a chance to hear the gospel, so finding the gate requires deliberate seeking. One must recognize their spiritual bankruptcy, repent, and believe in Christ's atonement. Most people are reluctant to seek and find it hard to accept Jesus as their Savior. Responding to the gospel may require forsaking friends and even family, facing significant resistance. However, it is essential to remember that entering the gate is receiving the free salvation offered by Christ on the cross 2000 years ago. Taking up the cross and following Him is part of discipleship and not a requirement to enter the narrow gate. Once inside, the path becomes easier to follow.

In summary, the two gates represent two distinct religious paths: the broad gate leading to destruction and the narrow gate leading to life. The broad gate is characterized by man's system, outward appearances, and self-righteousness, while the narrow gate involves a divine plan, inward change, and faith in Christ's atonement. Though few find the narrow gate, it offers the gift of salvation freely available through Jesus's sacrifice.

47. TWO FOUNDATIONS

In the Gospel of Matthew 7:24–27, Jesus imparts a profound lesson through the parable of the Two Foundations. This allegorical teaching unveils two distinct paths to salvation, symbolized by the rock and the sand. Through careful examination, we can glean essential insights into these foundations and their implications for our spiritual life.

Illustrations:
1) Two Houses: As Jesus concludes his Sermon on the Mount, He knows that there will be two responses. There are two men who built two houses. The two houses have a lot in common. In fact, from the outside, they may appear to have the same building despite one major difference.

2) Two Foundations: While the houses may look the same from the outside, there is something about them that is very different. Jesus tells us that the wise man builds his house on the rock while the foolish man builds his house on the sands.

1. **The Rock is Christ:** At the heart of this parable lies a pivotal truth: the Rock signifies Christ as the unshakable foundation for salvation. Just as a solid rock provides unwavering support for a building, so does Christ offer an unchanging and secure foundation for our faith. Through His sacrifice, resurrection, and divine grace, Jesus becomes the bedrock upon which we anchor our salvation. It is through faith in Him that we find forgiveness, redemption, and eternal life. As we delve deeper into the significance of this Rock, we unveil a profound invitation to build our lives on the unassailable truth of Christ's love and mercy.

    1) The Wise Man: He is the person who hears the words of Christ and obeys—and those who hear and obey are those who have built their lives on the foundation, which is Christ. The Scriptures often refer to Christ as a rock or a foundation, and this is the only rock that will be a sufficient foundation. Salvation is by faith. Faith comes by hearing, and hearing by the word of God (Rom. 10:17).

    2) The House That Stands: The hope of every person who hears and obeys the words of Christ is that they will be able to stand on the day of God's judgment and be welcomed into eternal life. Those who hear and obey are those who have Christ as their foundation. (1 Cor. 3:11)

2. **The Sand is Good Works:** Contrastingly, the sand represents the notion of relying solely on good works for salvation. While good deeds are undeniably important expressions of faith, this parable warns against placing our complete trust in them as the foundation of our salvation. Just as sand crumbles under pressure, the fleeting nature of human efforts cannot sustain our eternal destiny. This perspective challenges us to reflect on the intentions behind our actions and underscores the importance of aligning our deeds with the unwavering foundation of Christ's sacrifice.

   1) The foolish man: He builds his house on sand that will shift and move. This foundation is that of self-righteousness. This is the foundation that the religious leaders built on, and Jesus has made it clear that it will not be sufficient. Those who build on sand are those who have heard the word of Christ and do not obey (Matt. 13:18–23; Titus 1:6).

   2) The House That Falls: The fate of every person who hears and does not obey the words of Christ is that they will fall on the day of God's judgment, and the judgment will be eternal.

In the intricate tapestry of the parable of the Two Foundations, we discover a timeless lesson that transcends generations. As we navigate the complexities of life and faith, we are confronted with the choice between the rock of Christ's salvation and the sand of relying solely on good works. While good deeds undoubtedly have their place, the unshakable foundation of Christ beckons us to a deeper, more transformative understanding of salvation. By embracing Christ as our cornerstone, we stand firm amidst life's storms, fortified by His eternal love and grace. May we, like wise builders, choose to construct our lives on the enduring rock of Christ, for in Him alone do we find the steadfast assurance of salvation that surpasses the shifting sands of human endeavor.

48. TWO KINGDOMS

There is no real difference between the kingdom of God and the kingdom of heaven. The two phrases are simply two different ways to refer to the same thing: a kingdom or system of government that is ruled by God. Both are

The Assurance of Salvation

eternal kingdoms. But they are very different in nature and purpose. One is a spiritual kingdom, and the other is a physical kingdom.

1. **The Kingdom of God:** The kingdom of God is the rule and reign of God over all that exists. He reigns over the heavenly realm, the earth, the universe—over all that He created. Everything belongs to the Lord, and He is sovereign over all. The kingdom of God is a spiritual kingdom, unseen by the human eye. But we, as Christians, can "see" it with the "eyes of our understanding."

   The church age is the time since the cross, during which the Holy Spirit has sealed and indwells those who have come to faith in the Lord Jesus Christ. They have been forgiven of their sins and born again into the kingdom of God. The Holy Spirit is the "mark" of every citizen in the kingdom of God, and we understand Him to be the "guarantee" of our salvation and of all God's promises yet to come, including our living in the kingdom of heaven (the literal, physical place). As already stated, the kingdom of God is not seen. But it is here on earth, and it is a very real kingdom to every born-again believer.

   Luke 17:20–21 says, now when He was asked by the Pharisees when the kingdom of God would come, He answered them and said, "The Kingdom of God does not come with observation; nor will they say, 'See here!' or 'See there!' For indeed, the kingdom of God is within you." Our King enters our hearts and rules over our minds. Therefore, knowing that our King is a benevolent King, it should always be our desire to surrender to His will and obey His commands.

2. **The Kingdom of Heaven:** The kingdom of heaven is a literal, physical kingdom. It can be thought of as the place where God dwells in His glory. Since the fall in the garden, this kingdom has been in heaven, specifically in the third heaven (three heavens). There, God sits on the throne and rules over all, the spiritual and the physical kingdoms of which Christians are citizens of both. We certainly understand our being part of the spiritual kingdom, for it is the kingdom that we entered into when we were born again. It is a kingdom of "righteousness, and peace, and joy in the Holy Spirit" (Rom. 14:17). But we must always remember that we are also citizens of the kingdom of heaven.

The Kingdom of Heaven will be on earth. During Jesus's ministry, it was near. When Jesus taught, He preached, "the Kingdom of Heaven is at hand [near]" (Matt. 4:17), and He instructed His disciples to preach the same (Matt. 10:7). During the church age, this kingdom remains in the third heaven, where King Jesus sits on the throne. All born-again Christians will go there, at death or by rapture. And one day, Jesus will return to fulfill God's plan and purpose in restoring the earth:

1) Jesus will set up His kingdom on earth. Then new heaven and new earth.

2) He will rule and reign in righteousness from a new temple in Jerusalem, with His bride, the church, ruling with Him.

3) The Jews will be the lead nation in the kingdom of heaven on earth, and it will be a kingdom of righteousness and shalom (peace), similar to that which God created in the garden of Eden. The kingdom of heaven on earth is still in the future. It has not yet happened. But we know with all certainty that it will come to pass, just as God has promised in His Word.

In summary, the kingdom of God and the kingdom of heaven refer to the same divine rule and reign of God, emphasizing its spiritual nature and transformative impact on the world. They represent the present and future aspects of God's sovereign authority, with the hope and promise of God's ultimate victory over sin and evil. While the terms may have some contextual differences, they share a core understanding of God's reign as a central theme in Christian doctrine. Some have concluded that the kingdom of heaven includes true and false Christians, but the kingdom of God includes only true Christians (Millennium).

49. TWO NATURES

Humans consist of body/flesh and soul/spirit, which is how our physical bodies can perish, but we can still go on to live forever with Christ if we are believers. Galatians 5:16–26 is a biblical passage that discusses the contrast between the desires of the flesh and the fruit of the Spirit. In this passage, the apostle Paul writes to the Galatian church, emphasizing the importance of living a life led by the Spirit of God and not by the sinful desires of the flesh.

1. **The Flesh:** The fleshly or unregenerate person does not have the Holy Spirit. The Bible refers to this person as "the natural man." He is unable to discern the truths of God. This person lives according to the "old nature," "sinful nature," or "earthly nature" (Rom. 6:6; Col. 3:5).

    1) The "flesh" refers to the sinful nature or human tendency to rebel against God's will and indulge in sinful behaviors.

    2) It represents the selfish desires, passions, and cravings that can lead individuals away from God's intended path for their lives.

    3) Examples of "works of the flesh" mentioned in the passage include sexual immorality, impurity, idolatry, hatred, strife, jealousy, fits of anger, drunkenness, and other similar behaviors.

2. **The Spirit:** It is the Spirit of God that gives spiritual life to our human spirit. In order for the spiritual life to be ours, we must be born again (John 3:3).

    1) The "Spirit" refers to the Holy Spirit, the third person of the Holy Trinity, whom believers receive as a gift from God after accepting Jesus Christ as their Savior.

    2) When individuals are led by the Spirit, they experience transformation and demonstrate the "fruit of the Spirit" in their lives.

    3) The "fruit of the Spirit" mentioned in Galatians 5:22–23 includes love, joy, peace, patience, kindness, goodness, faithfulness, gentleness, and self-control.

The Battle between Flesh and Spirit (Rom. 7:15-25)

1) There is an ongoing internal struggle between the desires of the flesh and the leading of the Spirit in the life of a believer.

2) Paul urges the Galatians (and all believers) to walk in the Spirit, which means living in accordance with the guidance of the Holy Spirit and not giving in to the sinful desires of the flesh.

The Consequences:

1) The passage warns that those who consistently follow the desires of the flesh will not inherit the kingdom of God, as such behaviors are contrary to God's nature and His will for His children.

2) On the other hand, those who live by the Spirit will bear good fruit, which reflects a transformed and God-honoring life.

In summary, Galatians 5:16–26 teaches that followers of Christ should be led by the Holy Spirit and manifest the fruit of the Spirit in their lives. They are called to reject the desires of the flesh, which can lead to sinful behavior, and instead seek to live in obedience to God's Word and in alignment with His character. Through the power of the Holy Spirit, believers can overcome the desires of the flesh and experience true spiritual growth and transformation.

50. TWO LORDS

Jesus Christ and Satan, the two lords, one representing divine love, compassion, and salvation, and the other personifying temptation, darkness, and rebellion, stand as archetypal forces that have shaped the narratives of good and evil throughout history. As we delve into the complex duality of these figures, we unravel not only a tale of opposing ideologies but also a reflection of the human psyche itself. Through their contrasting roles, interactions, and symbolism, the enigmatic dance between Jesus Christ and Satan unveils profound insights into the eternal struggle between light and darkness.

1. **Jesus Christ:** Jesus Christ is the Son of God and the Messiah. God sent Him to earth to save humanity from sin and provide eternal life through his sacrifice on the cross. The phrase "every knee should bow; every tongue shall confess" is often associated with the idea that all will

acknowledge Jesus as Lord. Jesus is the King of kings and Lord of lords, and he will reign forever.

Jesus is for you. He loves you and desires the best for you. He loves you even more than He loves Himself. He proved it by dying in your place. He will give you eternal life as well as an abundant life. His desire is for you to have life in its fullness—life as God planned it to be—now and for all eternity.

Jesus is the Creator, and He is the way, the truth, and the life. Can you trust Jesus? The answer should be obvious. Anyone who cares for you enough to die in your place, suffering for you so you won't have to suffer, is trustworthy. Jesus promised to never forsake you. He will never quit loving you and trying to help you. Jesus said, "No man can serve two masters." (Matthew 6:24)

You need to invite and welcome Jesus Christ into your life—in every area. He wants to help you but will not force His help on you. If you don't, the devil may get into those areas of your life and wreak havoc (Luke 19:10; Phil. 2:10-11; John 10:10; Heb. 13:5; John 13:1).

2. **Satan** (Lucifer): Satan is often depicted as a fallen angel who rebelled against God and was cast out of heaven. He is often associated with deception, temptation, and evil. His malevolent nature and desire is to lead people away from God. Satan is the adversary of God and humanity, and he is ultimately destined to be cast into the lake of fire as a punishment for his rebellion.

The devil is the opposite of Jesus. The devil is against you and is always trying to steal from you, kill you, and destroy everything that is good. The devil is selfish and does not care about you or anyone else but himself.

Satan is the destroyer. He is a liar and a murderer. Can you trust the devil? Yes . . . to be the devil. You can depend on him lying and trying to always deceive you. The purpose of this deception is always to draw you away from God and His Word because that is your only source of help and deliverance from the devil's strategies, which is to blind the gospel to be veiled so that you are not able to receive the gospel of salvation. He is the god of this age and still active today. The trouble is that too many people hinder Jesus from saving them. They believe and follow what the devil says and turn away from Jesus and the Word of God (John 8:43-44; 10:10; 2 Cor. 4:3–4).

The eternal struggle between Jesus Christ and Satan transcends religious boundaries and resonates as a timeless metaphor for the human condition. As the embodiments of righteousness and malevolence, these two lords have challenged individuals and societies to confront their inner conflicts and navigate the intricate pathways of eternity.

51. TWO DEATHS

There are two kinds of deaths. "Spiritual death" can occur while a person is still physically alive. Without a connection to God, they may lead a life without true meaning, struggling with inner turmoil, and feeling alienated from the divine. Eternal death, often referred to as the "Second death" in the Bible, pertains to the ultimate fate of those who reject God and choose to remain in a state of spiritual death throughout their earthly lives. This results in eternal separation from God's presence and love. It is a state of permanent, unending separation from God and everything that is good, leading to eternal suffering and damnation.

1. **First Death - Spiritual Death**: This term refers to the state of being spiritually separated from God due to sin. It is mentioned in Ephesians 2:1, which states, "And you were dead in the trespasses and sins." Here, "dead" doesn't mean a physical death but a spiritual separation from God. It highlights the condition of humanity before coming to faith in Jesus Christ. People are spiritually dead, living in sin and separated from a right relationship with God. All human beings are born with a sinful nature inherited from Adam and Eve (original sin). As a result, they are spiritually dead, lacking the ability to restore their relationship with God on their own. However, through the redemptive work of Jesus Christ on the cross, people can receive forgiveness of sins and be spiritually reborn through faith in Him.

2. **Second Death - Eternal Death:** This term refers to the final judgment of the wicked as described in Revelation 20:14–15: "Then Death and Hades were thrown into the lake of fire. This is the second death. And anyone not found written in the Book of Life was cast into the lake of fire." The second death is the ultimate consequence of rejecting God's grace and living a life of unrepentant sin. It is eternal separation from God and punishment in the lake of fire, which is often equated with hell. This concept serves as a warning of the severe consequences of rejecting God's offer of salvation and choosing to persist in unbelief and rebellion against Him. In Matthew 10:28, Jesus emphasizes the eternal significance of the soul over the temporary nature of the physical body. It underscores the concept of divine judgment in the afterlife.

   1) Born Once - Die Twice: This statement suggests that those who are only born physically (born only of the flesh) but do not experience a spiritual rebirth (born of the spirit) will not be able to enter the kingdom of God. As a consequence, they will face a second death, which is mentioned in Revelation 20:15.

   2) Born Twice - Die Once: In contrast, this statement indicates that those who are born of the spirit (i.e., experience a spiritual rebirth) will enter the kingdom of God. Blessed and holy is he who has part in the first resurrection (second resurrection and second death are cursed). For them, the second death will have no power, as stated in Revelation 20:6.

In summary, the two deaths in Christian theology represent the state of spiritual separation from God due to sin (spiritual death) and the eternal consequence of rejecting God's salvation and living in unrepentant sin (second death). The second death is a solemn reminder of the need for reconciliation with God through faith in Jesus Christ, who offers the gift of eternal life to those who believe in Him.

52. TWO RESURRECTIONS

In the book of Daniel, specifically in Daniel 12:2, there is a compelling depiction of two distinct resurrections. This verse provides a glimpse into a future reality where individuals are awakened from death, each group destined for a different fate. The symbolism and interpretation surrounding these resurrections have sparked theological discussions and contemplation about the ultimate destiny of humanity.

1. **The First Resurrection** (Rev. 20:5–6 NIV): This speaks of the "first resurrection" and states, "Blessed and holy are those who share in the first resurrection. The second death has no power over them, but they will be priests of God and of Christ and will reign with him for a thousand years." The first resurrection refers to the resurrection of believers, those who have accepted Jesus Christ as their Lord and Savior and have a personal relationship with Him. According to this belief, those who participate in the first resurrection are considered blessed, and they will be granted eternal life in the presence of God. The first resurrection includes those who returned to life at the rapture. On the day of rapture, in the twinkling of an eye, a remarkable metamorphosis will occur. The perishable will give way to the imperishable, and mortality will be swallowed up by the splendor of immortality. As the apostle Paul eloquently articulates, "I declare to you, brothers and sisters, that flesh and blood cannot inherit the kingdom of God, nor does the perishable inherit the imperishable" (1 Cor. 15:50). This transformative event, often referred to as the blessed hope, holds profound significance in Christian eschatology (1 Thess. 4:13–17).

   The apostle's words carry a promise of divine magnificence. At the sounding of the heavenly trumpet, the dead in Christ shall rise first, their earthly bodies resurrected and gloriously transformed. Then, those who are alive and remain shall be caught up together with them in the clouds to meet the Lord in the air. This extraordinary meeting with the Lord signifies the culmination of earthly trials and the initiation of eternal fellowship. (The first resurrection takes place at the beginning of the thousand-year period.)

2. **The Second Resurrection** (Rev. 20:11–15): The second resurrection is associated with the fate of the non-believers or those who rejected God's salvation. This concept is mentioned in Revelation 20:15, which states, "And anyone not found written in the Book of Life was cast into the lake of fire." It is believed that this resurrection takes place after the millennial reign of Christ described in Revelation. Those who are part

of this resurrection will face judgment and ultimately be condemned to eternal separation from God, often referred to as the "second death" or being cast into the "lake of fire."

Daniel, Jesus, and the book of Revelation all speak of a resurrection of the wicked. It is said to be a resurrection unto shame and everlasting contempt. The Bible does not teach annihilation of the wicked. It teaches everlasting shame, contempt, and punishment. It is unthinkable what it would be like to be resurrected to stand before the Judge of all creation, knowing that we had rejected Him, spurned His offer of salvation, and now must face Him in judgment. What a contrast stands before us in these passages where we have looked at Daniel speaking of two resurrections and two destinies. (This second resurrection takes place at the end of the thousand-year period.)

The two resurrections described in Daniel 12:2 offer a captivating glimpse into the nature of human existence and the potential outcomes in the afterlife. Through the vivid imagery of those who "sleep in the dust of the earth" awakening to everlasting life or everlasting contempt, Daniel invites us to ponder the consequences of our actions and beliefs. Whether viewed through a religious lens or as a metaphor for personal transformation, these resurrections remind us of the eternal themes of justice, accountability, and the ultimate destiny that awaits us all. As we contemplate the meaning of these two resurrections, let us strive to lead lives of purpose, virtue, and compassion, seeking a path that aligns with the promise of a future beyond our mortal confines.

53. TWO DESTINATIONS

Central to the Christian concept of the afterlife is the idea that the final judgment is heaven and hell. According to Christian beliefs, there will be a day when all souls will be judged by God based on their relationship with Jesus Christ. Those who are deemed righteous and have accepted Christ will be granted entry into heaven, while those who have rejected God's grace and refused to repent will face eternal separation from Him in hell.

1. **The Description of Heaven:** Heaven is depicted as the eternal dwelling place of God and the blessed. It is described as a realm of perfect

happiness, peace, and communion with God. In heaven, believers experience the presence of God in all His glory and enjoy eternal life in His loving presence. It is a place of fulfillment, where all suffering, pain, and sorrow cease to exist. Entrance into heaven is granted to those who have faith in Jesus Christ. His life, death, and resurrection offer salvation and the forgiveness of sins. By accepting Jesus as their Lord and Savior, believers can have the hope of eternal life in heaven.

1) New Jerusalem (Rev. 21:2): In the Christian tradition, heaven is believed to be the eternal dwelling place of God and the righteous after death. It is often described as a place of eternal joy, peace, and communion with God. The New Jerusalem is mentioned as a heavenly city that descends from God, representing the ultimate dwelling place of believers. It is described as a place of great beauty, with precious stones, streets of gold, and no more pain or sorrow.

2) Paradise (Luke 23:43): The term "Paradise" appears in the Gospel of Luke in the context of Jesus's crucifixion. In Luke 23:43, Jesus is depicted as speaking to one of the criminals crucified alongside Him, promising him, "Assuredly, I say to you, today you will be with Me in Paradise." In this context, paradise refers to the immediate destination of the souls of the righteous who died before the resurrection of Jesus. It is often understood as a place of bliss and rest in the presence of God.

3) Abraham's Bosom (Luke 16:22): The concept of Abraham's bosom is mentioned in the parable of the rich man and Lazarus found in Luke 16:19–31. In this parable, Jesus tells the story of a rich man who ignored a poor beggar named Lazarus. Both the rich man and Lazarus die, and while the rich man is tormented in Hades, Lazarus is carried by angels to Abraham's bosom. Abraham's bosom symbolizes a place of comfort and blessing for the righteous after death, being in the presence of Abraham, the revered ancestor of the Jewish people.

2. **The Descriptions of Hell:** Hell is described as a place of eternal separation from God and is associated with suffering, torment, and punishment. It is depicted as a realm of darkness, where those who

have rejected God's offer of salvation and persisted in their rebellion against Him will face the consequences of their actions. God respects human freedom and grants individuals the choice to accept or reject Him. Those who reject God and live in rebellion against Him separate themselves from His love and choose to endure the consequences of that separation in hell.

In Mark 9:42–47, Jesus uses strong language to emphasize the seriousness of avoiding actions that can lead to negative consequences. The Bible tells us hell is a place of eternal punishment and suffering.

1) Gehenna: It is a term used in the New Testament, specifically in the Gospel of Matthew 5:22, where Jesus refers to it as a place of punishment. Gehenna originally referred to the Valley of Hinnom, a ravine outside Jerusalem, which became associated with idolatrous practices and human sacrifices in ancient times. It represents a place of eternal punishment and suffering. (MacArthur 2005, 1131).[24]

2) Sheol / Hades: "Sheol is a term found in the Hebrew Bible and is equivalent to the Greek term Hades. It refers to the realm of the dead or the grave, often depicted as a shadowy underworld. Sheol is not explicitly described as a place of punishment or torment but rather as a destination for all the deceased, where they exist in a state of shadowy existence or sleep" (Metzger and Coogan 1993, 277).[25]

3) Tartarus: It is a term mentioned in the New Testament, specifically in 2 Peter 2:4. It refers to a place of confinement or imprisonment for certain fallen angels or demons. In Greek mythology, Tartarus was a deep abyss beneath the underworld, reserved for the punishment of the wicked. In the biblical context, it represents a place of temporary punishment or confinement for rebellious supernatural beings. (Moo 1996, 103).[26]

4) Outer Darkness (Matt. 8:12): "But the sons of the kingdom will be cast out into outer darkness. There will be weeping and gnashing of teeth." Jesus responds to the faith of a Roman centurion. He contrasts the faith of the Gentile centurion with the lack of faith among

the people of Israel. The reference to "outer darkness" symbolizes a state of exclusion from the blessings of the kingdom of God, indicating a place of judgment and separation from God's presence.

5) Bottomless Pit (Rev. 9:2): The verse states: "And he opened the bottomless pit, and smoke arose out of the pit like the smoke of a great furnace. So the sun and the air were darkened because of the smoke of the pit." The "bottomless pit" is described as a place from which smoke and darkness emerge. It is associated with the unleashing of demonic forces and spiritual torment.

6) The Lake of Fire: It is mentioned in the book of Revelation 20:15. It is described as the final destination and eternal punishment for the wicked, including Satan, the beast, the false prophet, and those whose names are not found in the Book of Life. The lake of fire is depicted as a place of everlasting torment and separation from God.

Heaven and Hell represent the ultimate destination of spiritual consequence. Heaven is seen as a place of eternal peace, joy and closeness to the divine, reserved for those who have been born again. It symbolizes reward and eternal fulfillment. Hell, on the other hand, is depicted as a realm of suffering, punishment, and separation from the divine, meant for souls who have rejected Jesus Christ.

PART THREE

EXAMINE SCRIPTURE RELATED TO SALVATION

54. THE NOAH'S ARK

The story of Noah's ark (Gen. 6–8) stands as one of the most enduring and captivating stories in religious and cultural narratives. This ancient account, found within the pages of the book of Genesis, transcends its sacred origins to become a symbol of hope, faith, and resilience across various cultures. Rooted in themes of divine guidance, human responsibility, and the preservation of life, the story of Noah's ark continues to resonate with people of all ages and backgrounds. It serves as a powerful reminder of the capacity for renewal and the enduring connection between humanity and the natural world.

1. **Wickedness of the World and Its Wages** (Gen. 6:5–6): In the story of Noah's ark, we see how God observed the wickedness and corruption that had permeated the world. His decision to cleanse the earth through a flood reflects the serious consequences of sin. This aligns with the Christian teaching that sin leads to spiritual death and separation from God. As Romans 6:23a states, "For the wages of sin is death."

2. **Ark's Construction and the Death of Christ** (Gen. 6:14): The choice of materials used to construct the ark holds a symbolic significance. The ark was made from wood (not living trees), a material representing the death of Christ. Just as the ark's construction was necessary for survival from the flood, Christ's sacrificial death on the cross was essential for the forgiveness of sins. As Jesus explained in Luke 24:46, "Thus it is written, that the Christ should suffer and on the third day rise from

the dead." (Christ constructed a bridge using two wooden pieces [cross], connecting humanity with God.)

3. **Coated with Pitch and Eternal Security** (Gen. 6:14): The ark's unique feature of being coated inside and outside with pitch highlights the idea of perfect safety. Similarly, believers in Christ find their eternal security in Him. The parallel underscores the promise of Jesus in John 10:28: "And I give them eternal life, and they shall never perish; neither shall anyone snatch them out of My hand."

4. **Only One Door and One Way to Salvation** (Gen. 6:16): The ark's single door serves as a vivid representation of Christ as the exclusive pathway to salvation. Just as the ark had only one entrance, the Bible teaches that Jesus is the only door through which humanity can be saved. This concept is echoed in John 10:9, where Jesus says, "I am the door. If anyone enters by Me, he will be saved, and will go in and out and find pasture."

5. **Three Decks and Threefold Salvation** (Gen. 6:16): The ark's three decks correspond to a profound 'threefold salvation' for believers. First, passing from death to life symbolizes the spiritual rebirth that occurs when one accepts Christ. Second, having eternal life emphasizes the gift of everlasting life granted through faith. Third, escaping judgment reflects the assurance that believers will not face condemnation on the Day of Judgment. This threefold salvation aligns with Jesus's words in John 5:24.

6. **God's Invitation and Christ's Call** (Gen. 7:1): God's invitation to enter the ark during the flood finds resonance in Christ's own call to humanity. In the same way that God invited people into the ark for physical salvation, Jesus invites all to come to Him for spiritual salvation. Matthew 11:28 captures this invitation: "Come to me, all you who labor and are heavy laden, and I will give you rest."

7. **God's Wrath and Calvary's Redemption** (Gen. 7:11–12): The torrential rain lasting for forty days and nights in the flood narrative symbolizes God's righteous wrath. This parallels the concept of God's wrath being poured out on Calvary as Christ endured the cross for the

redemption of believers. As God's wrath was satisfied through Christ's sacrifice, believers are spared from condemnation. This connection is captured in Genesis 7:11–12 and finds fulfillment in Christ's work on the cross.

8. **Shutting Door and End of Grace Period** (Gen. 7:16): The moment when the Lord shut the door of the ark marks the conclusion of the grace period before the flood. This echoes the urgency of accepting salvation through Christ without delay. Just as the door of the ark closed, emphasizing the need to act promptly, 2 Corinthians 6:2b encourages us: "Behold, now is the accepted time; behold, now is the day of salvation."

9. **Two Groups of People – Those in Christ and Those Outside of Christ:** (Gen. 7:23) The clear distinction between those inside the ark and those outside it mirrors the spiritual division between those who are in Christ and those who remain outside His redemptive grace. Just as those inside the ark were protected from the flood's destruction, those in Christ find refuge from spiritual separation from God. These detailed explanations further highlight the intricate parallels between the story of Noah's ark and the profound truths of salvation through Jesus Christ.

10. **Covenant of Rainbow and New Covenant** (Gen. 9:13): God's covenant with the rainbow signifies His promise never to flood the entire earth again. This parallels the new covenant established through Jesus's sacrifice, where forgiveness of sins is offered to all who believe. As Hebrews 8:12 states, "For I will be merciful to their unrighteousness, and their sins and their lawless deeds I will remember no more."

Its themes of redemption, perseverance, and the value of life have kept it alive through the generations. The ark, constructed amidst divine guidance to weather an unprecedented cataclysm, serves as a testament to human determination and divine providence. Beyond its religious connotations, the narrative echoes the urgent need for environmental stewardship and compassion for all living beings. Just as the ark provided sanctuary in times of upheaval, this story encourages us to seek refuge in compassion, understanding, and unity, fostering a world where diversity is celebrated, and the bonds between all creatures are cherished.

55. THE SACRIFICE OF ISAAC

In Genesis 22:1–14, Abraham, often regarded as a representation of God the Father, plays a central role in this analogy. His willingness to obey God's command to sacrifice his beloved son, Isaac, mirrors the Father's ultimate plan to offer His own Son for the sake of humanity's redemption. Isaac, in this analogy, represents humanity as a whole—sinners in need of salvation. His innocence and submission to his father's will parallel the humility and surrender required for a sinner to accept God's plan of salvation.

1. **The Divine Command:** (vv. 1-2) God calls Abraham, a representation of God the Father, to sacrifice his beloved son, Isaac. This mirrors the Father's plan to offer His own Son for the redemption of humanity. Just as Abraham is willing to obey God's command, so, too, God the Father demonstrates his obedience to His redemptive plan.

2. **Isaac as Sinner:** (v. 6) Isaac, symbolizing humanity as a sinner, accompanies Abraham up the mountain. The weight of the wood he carries parallels the burden of human sin. Just as Isaac is unaware of the purpose of the journey, humanity often remains unaware of the depth of its sinfulness until confronted by the divine truth.

3. **The Wood, Fire, and Knife as God's Wrath:** (v. 7) The wood Isaac carries prefigures the wooden cross upon which Jesus, God the Son, would be crucified. The wood becomes a representation of humanity's sinful condition, which requires atonement. The fire and knife symbolize the wrath of God against sin. The fire signifies the righteous judgment of God's holiness, while the knife represents the impending punishment that sin deserves.

4. **All are spiritually bound:** (v. 9) As Abraham bound his son Isaac and placed him on the alter, symbolizing the gravity of sin, we, as human beings, are similarly bound by sin, and the consequence is death, the inevitable outcome of our sinful nature. "For God has bound everyone

over to disobedience so that he may have mercy on them all." (Rom. 11:32 NIV)

5. **The Lamb as God the Son:** (vv. 8, 13) Isaac asked the most important question of the world. "Where is the lamb of God for a burnt offering?" No other religions can answer it. Only Christ can. As Abraham prepares to sacrifice Isaac, God provides a ram caught in the thicket to be sacrificed in Isaac's place. This ram symbolizes Jesus, the Lamb of God. Just as the ram is a substitution for Isaac, Jesus becomes the ultimate substitution for humanity's sin. The ram is offered in place of Isaac, foreshadowing how Jesus would bear the penalty of sin on behalf of humanity.

6. **Jehovah Jireh - The Lord Provides:** (v. 14) The name "Jehovah Jireh" means "The Lord Will Provide". (Unger 1988, 782).[27] It is used in this story to emphasize how God provided the ram for the sacrifice, just as He provides salvation through Jesus Christ. This provision illustrates God's mercy and love for humanity, showcasing that He provides a way out of the consequences of sin.

7. **Redemption and Sacrifice:** The story concludes with God reaffirming His covenant with Abraham and blessing him. This echoes the promise of salvation and blessings that come through the sacrifice of Jesus Christ. The analogy encapsulates the concept of redemption, where God's mercy triumphs over His wrath, and humanity's sin is pardoned through the ultimate sacrifice.

Ultimately, the sacrifice of Isaac serves as a poignant foreshadowing of the redemptive plan that God would fulfill through Jesus Christ. The story underscores the profound love and mercy of God, who provides a way for humanity to be reconciled to Him despite their sinful nature. It demonstrates the intricate interplay of divine justice and divine mercy, showcasing the lengths to which God would go to bring about the salvation of humanity. In this detailed analysis of the analogy, each element of the story represents a profound theological concept. The sacrifice of Isaac encapsulates the themes of obedience, substitutionary sacrifice, atonement, divine justice, mercy, and God's redemptive plan. Through these parallels, the narrative highlights the intricate plan of salvation that God orchestrates throughout history, ultimately leading to the sacrificial death and resurrection of Jesus Christ.

56. REBECCA

In this particular narrative from the Bible (Gen. 27:1–29), the characters embody profound symbolic meanings. Isaac, one of the central figures, serves as a representation of God the Father. Likewise, Rebecca takes on the role of a symbol for God the Son. The intricate layers of this allegory continue with Jacob, who is emblematic of the redeemed sinner. Finally, Esau emerges as a poignant depiction of the lost sinner. This story, replete with such metaphorical significance, underscores the intricate interplay of spiritual themes within the narrative. Here's a breakdown of each point:

1. **Jacob's Obedience and Hearing Christ's Saying** (Gen. 27:8; Matt. 7:24): In the story, Jacob had to obey Rebecca's instructions in order to receive the blessings that were meant for his brother Esau. This parallelizes with the idea that believers need to hear and follow Christ's teachings to build their spiritual foundation on solid ground, just as the wise man built his house on the rock in the parable taught by Jesus (Matt. 7:24). The obedience demonstrated by Jacob reflects the importance of adhering to Christ's words for salvation.

2. **Rebecca's Savory Food and Christ's Sacrifice** (Gen. 27:10; Eph. 5:2): Rebecca prepared savory food to symbolically win Isaac's favor and blessings for Jacob. This is analogous to Christ's sacrifice on the cross, where He offered Himself as a pleasing and sweet-smelling sacrifice to God for the salvation of humanity (Eph. 5:2). The parallel emphasizes Christ's sacrificial act as the ultimate expression of love and redemption.

3. **Taking on the Curse and Christ's Redemption** (Gen. 27:12; Gal. 3:13): Jacob feared the curse that could result from deceiving his father, but Rebecca offered to take the curse upon herself. This mirrors Christ's redemptive act on the cross, where He bore the curse of the law on behalf of humanity, offering redemption from the curse (Gal. 3:13). Rebecca's willingness to bear the curse symbolizes Christ's substitutionary sacrifice for believers' salvation.

4. **Putting on Choice Clothes and Putting on Christ** (Gen. 27:15; Gal. 3:26–27): Rebecca put Esau's choice clothes on Jacob to enable him to receive the blessings. This parallels the concept of believers putting on Christ's righteousness through faith. Just as Jacob's appearance changed through the choice clothes, believers' spiritual identity changes when they put on Christ (Gal. 3:26–27). The imagery highlights the transformation that occurs through salvation.

5. **Exchange of Sin and Righteousness** (Gen. 27:16; 2 Cor. 5:21): Rebecca covered Jacob's hands and neck with the skins of goat kids to mimic the appearance of Esau's hairy skin. This exchange is likened to Christ's exchange of His sinless nature for the sins of humanity on the cross. Through this exchange, believers are made righteous before God (2 Cor. 5:21). The parallel underscores the concept of imputed righteousness.

6. **Offering of Flesh and Blood for Salvation** (Gen. 27:27; John 6:53–54): Jacob presented savory food and wine to Isaac by the will of his mother, seeking his blessings. Similarly, Christ offered His own flesh and blood as a means of salvation. In the Last Supper, Jesus used bread and wine to symbolize His body and blood, which provide spiritual nourishment and eternal life for believers (John 6:53–54).

7. **Isaac's Eyes were dim ... Hidden with Christ for Salvation** (Gen. 27:1, Col. 3:3): Isaac's blindness to Jacob's deception corresponds to the idea of believers being hidden with Christ. In Colossians 3:3, believers are told that their lives are hidden with Christ in God. This reflects the idea that believers are spiritually united with Christ and find their identity, security, and salvation in Him.

In all these parallels, the intention is to draw connections between the events in the Old Testament narrative and the spiritual truths and concepts found in the New Testament teachings of Christ's sacrifice and salvation. This type of allegorical interpretation helps believers understand the deeper meanings and significance of these stories within the broader framework of God's redemptive plan.

57. PASSOVER LAMB

The analogy between the Passover lamb in the Old Testament, particularly in Exodus 12:1-13, and Jesus Christ in the New Testament is a significant theme in Christian theology. In the Passover story, the Israelites were enslaved in Egypt, and God instructed them to sacrifice a lamb without blemish and spread its blood on their doorposts. This act of obedience marked the houses so that the angel of death would "pass over" those homes, sparing the firstborn sons inside. This Passover event foreshadowed the ultimate sacrifice that was fulfilled in Jesus Christ. In the New Testament, Jesus is often referred to as the "Lamb of God." Just as the "Passover lamb" was without blemish, Jesus, as the sinless Son of God, was the perfect and unblemished sacrifice for the sins of humanity.

1. **Setting the Context** (vv. 1–6): In Exodus 12, God is about to execute the tenth and final plague upon Egypt—the death of the firstborn. He instructs the Israelites on how to prepare for this event and escape its consequences. Jesus is the Passover Lamb (1 Cor. 5:7).

2. **Selection of the Lamb** (vv. 3–4): God commands each household to select a lamb without blemish or defect, a male of the first year. This lamb would symbolize purity and innocence. Similarly, in the New Testament, Jesus is described as the sinless and blameless Lamb of God (1 Pet. 2:22; John 1:29).

3. **The Lamb's Sacrifice** (v. 5): On the fourteenth day of the first month, the Israelites are to slaughter the lamb at twilight. The lamb's blood is to be collected in a basin. This blood serves as a protective mark on the doorposts and lintel of their houses. In Christianity, Jesus's crucifixion is seen as a sacrificial act, where His blood atones for the sins of humanity.

4. **Applying the Blood of the Lamb** (vv. 7, 13): The lamb's blood is applied to the doorposts and lintel of the Israelites' homes. When the Lord passes through Egypt to strike down the firstborn, He will "pass over" the houses with the blood on the doorposts. This represents God's act of salvation for those covered by the lamb's blood. In the same way,

Jesus's sacrifice on the cross provides salvation for those who trust in Him. (1 Pet. 1:18-19)

5. **Eating the flesh of the Lamb** (v. 8): God instructs the Israelites to roast the lamb and eat it with unleavened bread and bitter herbs. This meal represents a communion between God and His people, a shared experience of deliverance. In the New Testament, Jesus institutes the Lord's Supper (Holy Communion) as a symbolic representation of His body and blood, emphasizing the spiritual connection and redemption. The roasted flesh and bitter herbs represent his suffering on the cross for the deliverance of humanity from sin and death. (John 6:53)

6. **Ever Ready for Departure** (v. 11): They had to eat the Passover feast in haste. During the account of the first Passover, God instructs the Israelites to eat the Passover meal with a sense of urgency, being fully prepared to depart from Egypt. This meal was to be eaten quickly and with their loins girded, sandals on their feet, and staff in hand, ready to leave at a moment's notice. Just as the Israelites had to be ready to leave Egypt quickly, believers are encouraged to be spiritually vigilant and prepared for our departure from this world. (2 Cor. 6:2)

7. **Departure to Freedom** (vv. 12–13): That very night, God executes judgment on Egypt, and the Israelites are set free from bondage. The blood of the lamb has secured their liberation. The Passover becomes an annual commemoration of this event. Similarly, in Christianity, Jesus's sacrifice leads to freedom from the bondage of sin and eternal separation from God.

8. **Significance for Christians:** The analogy of the Passover lamb as Christ Jesus emphasizes several key themes:

    1) Substitutionary Atonement: Just as the lamb's blood protected the Israelites from the judgment of death, Jesus's blood offers forgiveness and salvation to believers.

    2) Innocent Sacrifice: The lamb was without blemish, symbolizing purity. Likewise, Jesus was sinless and offered Himself as a blameless sacrifice for humanity's sins.

3) **Deliverance and Freedom:** The Israelites' liberation from slavery parallels the spiritual freedom that believers gain through Christ's sacrifice.

4) **Covenant Relationship:** The Passover meal represents a covenant relationship between God and His people. Similarly, Christians partake in communion to strengthen their relationship with God.

9. **The Effective Significance of the Passover Lamb's Blood:** It can be understood as follows: Firstly, the blood within a living lamb symbolizes the incarnation of Christ. Secondly, the blood placed in a bowl represents Christ's sacrificial death on the cross. Lastly, the blood applied to the doorposts and lintel signifies the cleansing through Christ's blood by accepting Him as one's Savior and Lord. It's important to note that only the third aspect leads to salvation.

In summary, the analogy of the Passover Lamb in Exodus 12:1–13 serves as a powerful foreshadowing of Christ's redemptive work, highlighting themes of substitutionary atonement, innocence, deliverance, and covenant relationship.

58. THE BRAZEN SERPENT

The narrative of the Brazen Serpent, found in Numbers 21:4–9 of the Old Testament, is a poignant and symbolic episode within the biblical account of the Israelites' journey through the wilderness. This passage sheds light on the complex relationship between faith, obedience, and divine mercy. As the Israelites grapple with their frustrations and doubts, they encounter a profound lesson about repentance and salvation. The story of the Brazen Serpent serves as a reminder of the intricate interplay between human frailty and the boundless grace of a compassionate God.

1. **The Israelites' Transgression** (vv. 4–5): In this passage, it is recounted that the Israelites, while journeying through the wilderness, grew weary and impatient due to the hardships of their journey. This impatience led them to speak against both God and Moses. Their discontent and

EXAMINE SCRIPTURE RELATED TO SALVATION

complaints were considered a transgression against the divine plan and their chosen leaders.

2. **The Divine Punishment** (v. 6): As a response to the Israelites' murmuring and complaints, God allowed venomous snakes to enter the camp, resulting in a plague of deadly snake bites. The affliction served as a punishment for their lack of faith and their disobedience toward God's guidance.

3. **The Israelites' Repentance** (v. 7): Realizing the gravity of their actions and the dire consequences that befell them, the Israelites acknowledged their sin and repented. They approached Moses, acknowledging their wrongdoing and seeking his intercession to entreat God's mercy on their behalf.

4. **God's Intervention and Mercy** (v. 8): Upon witnessing the sincerity of the Israelites' repentance and their plea for relief, God instructed Moses to craft a bronze serpent and place it on a pole. Those who were bitten by the poisonous snakes were told to look at the bronze serpent. By doing so, they would experience healing and be spared from the deadly effects of the snakebites. This act of mercy from God demonstrated his willingness to provide a solution for their affliction.

5. **The Remedy for the Israelites** (v. 9): Following God's command, Moses fashioned the bronze serpent and raised it on a pole in the midst of the camp. Those who had been bitten and gazed upon the bronze serpent experienced miraculous healing. The bronze serpent, in this context, symbolized God's divine remedy for the affliction that had befallen the Israelites, highlighting the importance of faith and obedience.

6. **Parallel** (John 3:14–15): In the Gospel of John, Jesus referred to the story of the Brazen Serpent as a metaphorical parallel to his own redemptive mission. Just as the Israelites looked upon the bronze serpent to be healed from their physical affliction, Jesus explained that whoever believes in him will have eternal life. Just as the bronze serpent served as a symbol of healing and salvation, Jesus saw himself as the ultimate means of salvation, emphasizing the importance of faith in his redemptive work.

The Assurance of Salvation

7. Two Groups of People

I. Those who do not look at the serpent (Bad news for non-believers)

(1) Even one bite from a snake caused death (Rom. 5:16a)
(2) Even a small bite resulted in death (Matt. 12:36-37)
(3) The location, whether on the head or legs, do not matter; they would die (Rom. 6:23a)
(4) Even if they tried their best to treat the snake bite, they would die (1 Cor. 15:22a)

II. Those who look at the serpent (Good news for believers)
(1) They would live even if they have many bites (Rom. 5:16b)
(2) They would live even if the bite is very serious (1 Tim. 1:15)
(3) They would live regardless of where the snake bit them (Rom. 6:23b)
(4) They would live, even if they did nothing else to treat the bite (1 Cor. 15:23b)

In Numbers 21:4–9, the account of the Brazen Serpent remains a timeless metaphor for redemption and spiritual healing. Through this incident, we witness the consequences of doubt and rebellion, yet we also discover the limitless mercy of God who provides a way out of suffering. The uplifted serpent, a symbol of Christ's eventual crucifixion, becomes a means of salvation for those who gaze upon it in faith. This narrative invite reflection on our own struggles and the transformative power of faith and obedience in the face of adversity. Just as the Israelites found deliverance by turning their eyes to the Brazen Serpent, so, too, can we find solace and renewal through our unwavering trust in a compassionate and forgiving Creator.

59. JONAH

The book of Jonah in the Bible tells the story of a prophet named Jonah and his journey of running away from God, facing various challenges, and ultimately learning important lessons about God's mercy and compassion. The book is divided into four chapters, each representing different aspects of Jonah's relationship with God. Let's delve into each chapter in detail:

EXAMINE SCRIPTURE RELATED TO SALVATION

1. **Jonah Runs from God** (Chapter 1): In this chapter, God commands Jonah to go to the city of Nineveh and deliver a message of repentance to the people there. However, Jonah disobeys God's command and tries to escape by boarding a ship headed in the opposite direction, toward Tarshish. He's essentially running away from his divine calling. God sends a great storm upon the sea as a consequence of Jonah's disobedience. The sailors on the ship eventually discover that Jonah is the cause of the storm, and realizing his actions have provoked God's anger, Jonah tells them to throw him into the sea to calm the storm. Jonah's actions in this chapter highlight his attempt to escape God's will and his resistance to fulfilling his prophetic mission.

2. **Jonah Runs to God** (Chapter 2): After being thrown into the sea, a great fish or whale swallows Jonah. Inside the belly of the fish, Jonah prays a heartfelt prayer of repentance and cries out to God for help. This chapter shows Jonah's turning point, as he realizes the gravity of his disobedience and seeks reconciliation with God. He acknowledges his mistake and promises to fulfill his original mission to go to Nineveh. The time spent in the belly of the fish serves as a period of reflection and spiritual transformation for Jonah.

3. **Jonah Runs with God** (Chapter 3): In this chapter, the fish vomits Jonah onto dry land, and God once again commands him to go to Nineveh and deliver the message of repentance. This time, Jonah obeys God's command and travels to Nineveh, a great city known for its wickedness. He proclaims the impending judgment of God, and to Jonah's surprise, the people of Nineveh, including the king, respond with genuine repentance. They fast, put on sackcloth, and turn away from their sinful ways. God sees their repentance and chooses not to bring the foretold destruction upon Nineveh. This chapter reflects the concept of running alongside God, as Jonah is now aligned with God's plan and witnesses the positive outcomes of obedience and repentance.

4. **Jonah Runs before God** (Chapter 4): In the final chapter, Jonah's attitude takes a turn again. He becomes upset and angry because God has shown mercy to the people of Nineveh rather than bringing destruction upon them. Jonah goes outside the city and constructs a makeshift shelter to watch what will happen to Nineveh. God causes a plant to

grow and provide shade for Jonah, which makes him happy. However, when God sends a worm to destroy the plant and the sun beats down on Jonah, he becomes even angrier and wishes for death. God uses this situation to teach Jonah a lesson about compassion and mercy. God's response highlights that He cares for all His creations, including the people of Nineveh. This chapter reveals Jonah's struggle to fully understand and embrace God's attributes of compassion and forgiveness.

In summary, the story of Jonah is a narrative of spiritual growth and understanding, as Jonah goes through various stages of running away from God's call, seeking reconciliation, aligning with God's purpose, and grappling with his own biases and judgments. The book teaches important lessons about obedience, repentance, God's mercy, and the complexity of human emotions and attitudes.

60. MEPHIBOSHETH

2 Samuel 9: At the beginning of the chapter, David has established his rule as king over all Israel. He remembers his covenant with his dear friend Jonathan, who was the son of King Saul. Jonathan had died in battle, and David wants to show kindness to Jonathan's descendants as a way of fulfilling his promise.

This story of David's kindness to Mephibosheth for Jonathan's sake can be seen as an analogy for God's love for sinners through Jesus Christ.

1. **David Represents God:** (v. 1) David's mercy and kindness toward Mephibosheth reflect God's unconditional love for sinners. Despite Mephibosheth's unworthiness, David reaches out to him just as God reaches out to sinful humanity.

2. **Mephibosheth Represents Sinners:** (v. 3) Mephibosheth's physical condition and his lineage (grandson of Saul) symbolize the brokenness and spiritual destitution of humanity due to sin. Like Mephibosheth, (who is lame in his feet) we are unable to come to God on our own.

3. **David's Covenant with Jonathan:** (1 Sam. 18:3) Just as David remembered his covenant with Jonathan, God remembers His covenant with

humanity through Jesus Christ. God's promise of salvation and forgiveness is fulfilled through Christ's sacrifice on the cross.

4. **The Place Where Mephibosheth Lived** (v. 5): Lo Debar was a town located east of the Jordan River and north of Mahanaim. The name 'Lo Debar' means 'no pasture' or 'nothing' in Hebrew. (Unger 1988, 780).[28] This place is often interpreted symbolically to signify barrenness, lack, or desolation. It's depicted as our spiritual world where we live now.

5. **Mephibosheth's Humble Response:** (v. 8) Mephibosheth's humility before David reflects the repentant attitude of a sinner coming to God. Acknowledging our unworthiness and receiving God's grace with humility is essential for a restored relationship.

6. **Restoration and Relationship:** (v. 9) Just as Mephibosheth was restored to Saul's inheritance and brought into David's family, sinners are offered restoration, forgiveness, and adoption into God's family through Christ. (Col. 1:21, Eph. 1:5)

7. **Invitation to the King's Table:** (v. 11) David's invitation to Mephibosheth is a powerful example of his complex character and his desire to emulate God's own heart (1 Sam. 13:14). Despite the military rhetoric in 2 Samuel 5:8, David's true nature shines through in his merciful actions towards Mephibosheth. David's invitation to dine at the king's table represents God's invitation for sinners to enter a restored relationship with Him through Jesus. The "table" symbolizes fellowship, intimacy, and grace. (Rev. 3:20, Luk. 14:15-24)

8. **Dwelling in Jerusalem:** (v. 13) Mephibosheth's dwelling in Jerusalem signifies the place of honor and security in God's presence that believers can experience through faith in Christ. 2 Samuel 9 illustrates how David's compassion and kindness to Mephibosheth mirror God's immense love and grace extended to sinners through the sacrifice of Jesus Christ, leading to a restored relationship and a place of honor in God's kingdom.

The story of David and Mephibosheth highlight theme of loyalty, kindness, and redemption. Mephibosheth the lame son of Jonathan was shown

The Assurance of Salvation

unexpected mercy by David, who honored his covenant with Jonathan by restoring Mephibosheth's inheritance and granting him a place at the king's table. Despite his physical limitations and the potential political threat he posed as a descendant of Saul, Mephibosheth experienced David's compassion, reflecting the king's commitment to justice and loyalty beyond personal gain. This act underscores the power of grace and covenantal faithfulness.

61. THE CITIES OF REFUGE

In Joshua 20, Numbers 35:9–28 and Deut. 19:1-13 we encounter a concept known as the "cities of refuge." These were a set of cities established by God's command for the Israelites as a means of providing refuge and protection for individuals who unintentionally caused the death of another person. The cities of refuge were designed to prevent blood feuds and ensure that justice was carried out fairly. There were six cities of refuge in total, strategically located across the land of Israel.

1. **The Source Is God:** (Josh. 20:1) Just as the cities of refuge were established by God's command, the provision of salvation and refuge comes from God through Christ. Christ is the means through which salvation is offered.

2. **The Necessity:** (Josh. 20:3) In the case of the cities of refuge, there was a necessity to provide a safe haven for those who had accidentally taken someone's life. Similarly, in Christianity, there is a necessity for a savior due to the fallen nature of humanity and our separation from God due to sin.

3. **Accidental Sin and Guilt:** (Josh. 20:5) Just as individuals in ancient Israel might have accidentally taken a life, people today find themselves ensnared in the consequences of their own sins. Sin is often seen as unintentional actions or decisions that lead to spiritual death and separation from God. In the same way, the cities of refuge were meant for those who had committed unintentional acts resulting in death.

4. **The Cities:** (Josh. 20: 7-8) These cities were Kedesh, Shechem, Hebron, Bezer, Ramoth, and Golan. The idea behind these cities was that if

someone accidentally killed another person, they could flee to one of these cities and seek asylum. The accused individual would stand trial in front of the local assembly to determine whether the killing was accidental or intentional. If deemed accidental, they would be given protection within the city walls, shielded from the vengeance of the victim's family.

5. **The Scope Is All:** (Josh. 20:9) The cities of refuge were available to all who needed them. Similarly, Christ's salvation is available to all people, regardless of their background or circumstances.

6. **Its Accessibility:** (Deut. 19:3) The cities of refuge were strategically located so that they could be accessed relatively easily. Similarly, Christ's salvation is accessible to all who seek it through faith.

7. **Its Security:** (Deut. 19:4) The cities of refuge provided a secure place for those inside, protecting them from avengers. Likewise, Christ provides security and protection for believers from the consequences of sin in Him alone.

8. **The Need for Protection:** (Deut. 19:5) Sinners, like those seeking refuge in the cities of refuge, require a place of safety. In the spiritual sense, people need protection from the consequences of their sins and the impending judgment that sin brings. Christ offers this protection through His sacrificial death and resurrection.

9. **Seeking Asylum:** (Deut. 19:10) Just as the person who accidentally killed another sought refuge within the city of refuge, sinners are called to seek refuge in Christ. This involves acknowledging their sins, repenting, and turning to Christ for forgiveness and salvation.

10. **Protection from Vengeance:** (Josh. 20:3) Christ, analogous to the cities of refuge, offers protection from the eternal consequences of sin. Believers find security in Christ's atoning sacrifice and His promise of salvation. Just as the accused in the cities of refuge were protected from the avenger of blood, believers in Christ are protected from the wrath of God.

11. **The Trial and Verdict:** (Josh. 20:6) In the cities of refuge, a trial took place to determine the intention behind the act. Similarly, through faith in Christ, believers undergo a transformational process where their sins are brought to light and they experience God's forgiveness and grace. This spiritual process serves to bring about genuine repentance and transformation.

12. **Shelter in Christ:** (Josh. 20:4) The image of the cities of refuge illustrates the concept of finding shelter in Christ. Just as the cities of refuge were designated safe havens, Christ is the ultimate refuge where sinners can find forgiveness, redemption, and eternal life.

13. **Its Provision:** (Josh. 20:6; Num. 35:32) In the case of the cities of refuge, safety was only guaranteed as long as the high priest lived. Similarly, in the analogy with Christ, believers are safe and secure due to the sacrificial death and resurrection of Jesus Christ, our eternal High Priest. We are secured eternally as our Savior lives forever.

Drawing this analogy helps to underscore the significance of Christ's role as our Refuge and Savior. Just as the cities of refuge offered safety and protection from those seeking vengeance, Christ offers us salvation and reconciliation with God, shielding us from the consequences of sin. The analogy emphasizes the essential aspects of Christ's provision and the security found in Him, paralleling the safety found within the cities of refuge when the high priest was alive.

62. NAAMAN

Today, we gather to delve into a profound story of healing, redemption, and the transformative power of faith (2 Kings 5:1–19). Our analogy sermon takes us back to ancient times, to the story of Naaman, a valiant commander afflicted with leprosy who found healing in the waters of the Jordan River. In this narrative, we discover a powerful analogy to our own spiritual journey of being cleansed and redeemed by the blood of Jesus Christ.

1. **The Affliction of Naaman and the Leprosy of Sin:** (v. 1) We are introduced to Naaman, a mighty commander esteemed by his people but plagued by a debilitating disease: leprosy. Just as Naaman was afflicted

physically, we, too, are burdened by a spiritual leprosy—sin. Sin separates us from God, taints our hearts, and weakens our souls, preventing us from experiencing the fullness of life that God intends for us.

2. **The Path to Healing:** (vv. 2-3) In this narrative, a servant girl captured from Israel shares the message of hope with Naaman's wife. She tells them of a prophet in Samaria who could heal Naaman's leprosy. Similarly, God sent us a message of hope—the gospel—through His Son Jesus Christ. Just as the servant girl pointed Naaman toward a solution, we, born-again believers, share this good news to people toward the path of redemption and healing.

3. **The Humble Journey:** (vv. 9–12) Naaman's Journey to the Jordan: Naaman, initially reluctant, humbles himself and follows the prophet Elisha's instructions to wash in the Jordan River seven times. This act of humility and obedience was pivotal in his healing. In our own spiritual journey, we must humble ourselves before God, recognizing our need for His forgiveness and salvation. Just as Naaman had to follow Elisha's guidance, we must follow Jesus's teachings and submit ourselves to His will.

4. **The Cleansing Waters:** (vv. 13-14) Healing through Obedience: As Naaman immersed himself in the Jordan's waters, he was cleansed of his leprosy. This healing was not brought about by the waters themselves but by his obedience and faith in the process. Similarly, it is not the waters of the Jordan that cleanse us but the blood of Jesus shed on the cross. Our repentance and faith in Christ's sacrifice allow us to be cleansed from the leprosy of sin.

5. **Redemption through Sacrifice:** The Blood of Jesus: Naaman's healing was a result of his obedience and faith, just as our redemption is made possible through Jesus's sacrifice on the cross. In Romans 5:8 NIV, we are reminded that "God demonstrates His own love for us in this: While we were still sinners, Christ died for us." The blood of Jesus has the power to wash away our sins, making us new and pure before God. (1 John 1:7b)

6. **Salvation Is a Divine Gift:** (vv. 15-16) It is freely given without any requirement for payment or compensation. This fundamental concept is beautifully illustrated in the story of Naaman's healing as recounted in the biblical narrative. In this way, the story of Naaman's healing and Elisha's refusal of the gift underscores the spiritual truth that salvation is a gift that cannot be earned, purchased, or exchanged. It is a reflection of God's unmerited favor and a testament to the limitless love and grace that He extends to humanity.

The story of Naaman's healing and redemption is a profound analogy for our own spiritual journey. Just as Naaman was cleansed from his leprosy through humble obedience, we can be cleansed from our sins through faith in the sacrifice of Jesus. Let us embrace the message of hope, submit ourselves in humility, and find healing in the cleansing waters of Christ's blood. As we reflect on this powerful analogy, may we renew our commitment to follow Jesus, the ultimate source of redemption and eternal life. Amen.

63. THE FLOATING AX

This is a story that speaks to the vulnerabilities of human nature, the power of faith, and the unexpected ways in which divine intervention can shape the course of history. The account of the "Fallen Ax Head," as recorded in 2 Kings 6:1–7, unveils a moment of crisis and the miraculous response that highlights the interplay between human effort and the supernatural. This story invites us to ponder the depths of faith and the limitless capacity of the divine to transform even the direst circumstances into displays of grace and wonder.

1. **Context and Setting:** (vv. 1-3) The passage takes place during the time of the prophet Elisha. The "sons of the prophets," who were likely his disciples or followers, wanted to expand their living quarters and decided to gather logs by the Jordan River to build a new dwelling place.

2. **Cutting Down Trees:** (v. 4) The disciples go to the Jordan River to cut down trees for construction. This action can be seen as representative of humanity's efforts to construct a life for themselves, symbolizing the earthly pursuits and endeavors that people engage in.

3. **The Falling Ax-Head:** (v. 5) While one of the disciples is chopping down a tree, the iron ax-head attached to the handle falls into the water. This unexpected event represents the fall of mankind, referring to the biblical narrative of Adam and Eve's disobedience in the garden of Eden, which led to humanity's separation from God and the entrance of sin into the world.

4. **The Cry for Help:** (v. 5) The disciple who lost the ax-head cries out in distress because the ax-head was borrowed, indicating a sense of responsibility and accountability for what has been lost. This can be interpreted as humanity's realization of the consequences of sin and their need for redemption.

5. **Elisha's Response:** (v. 6) Elisha, the "man of God," intervenes to help. His role can be likened to that of Christ, who comes to rescue and restore humanity. Elisha asks where the ax-head fell, directing attention to the specific place of the fall, paralleling how Christ's redemptive work is targeted toward the specific issue of sin.

6. **The Floating Ax-Head:** (v. 6) Elisha cuts off a stick and throws it into the water at the place where the ax-head fell. The miraculous event that follows, where the iron ax-head floats to the surface, can be seen as an analogy for salvation through Christ's sacrifice on the cross. Just as the ax-head defies the laws of nature by floating, humanity's salvation through Christ's sacrifice defies the spiritual consequences of sin.

7. **Taking Up the Ax-Head:** (v. 7) Elisha instructs the disciple to take up the floating ax-head. This action signifies the recovery and restoration of what was lost. Similarly, Christ's sacrifice offers salvation and the possibility of reconciliation between humanity and God. Since salvation is God's free gift, the moment you accept Jesus Christ as your Savior, the salvation is already yours.

The narrative of the fallen ax-head found in 2 Kings 6:1–7 serves as an enduring testament to the belief that faith and humility can ignite divine intervention in the midst of life's challenges. Through the prophet Elisha's intercession, we witness the extraordinary transformation of a seemingly insurmountable problem into a remarkable miracle. This account reminds us that even when we find ourselves faced with adversity, there exists a wellspring of hope rooted in our connection to the divine. The tale of the fallen ax-head beckons us to seek guidance in our times of need, believe in the extraordinary, and recognize that ordinary tools and circumstances can become vessels for extraordinary grace. Just as the iron ax-head floated, defying the laws of nature, our faith can elevate us above the limitations of our circumstances, allowing us to discover the profound depths of God's mercy and provision.

64. JOSHUA, THE PRIEST

In Zechariah 3:1–5, the prophet Zechariah receives a vision that portrays a symbolic scene involving Joshua the high priest and an angel of the Lord. This vision is often interpreted as a representation of spiritual renewal, cleansing, and God's forgiveness for the people of Israel. Let's break down the passage:

1. **Joshua the High Priest:** (v. 1) Joshua represents the people of Israel, particularly the priestly aspect of the nation. His role as the high priest makes him a significant figure in the religious leadership of Israel.

2. **The Angel of the LORD:** (v. 1) The angel of the LORD in this passage is a divine messenger, possibly a preincarnate appearance of Jesus Christ. This figure intervenes on behalf of Joshua and the people of Israel.

3. **Satan's Accusation:** (v. 2) Satan stands as the accuser, pointing out the sins and transgressions of Joshua and, by extension, the people of Israel. This highlights the spiritual opposition and accusations that come against God's people. (Rev. 12:10)

4. **Rebuke and Redemption:** (v. 2) When the LORD rebukes Satan, it emphasizes God's authority over the accuser and the accused. The mention of Joshua as a "brand plucked from the fire" suggests God's mercy and intervention to save him despite his sinful state. (Jude 1:9)

5. **Filthy Garments:** (v. 3) The filthy garments that Joshua is clothed in symbolize the spiritual impurity and sinfulness of the people of Israel.

It reflects their collective disobedience and unrighteousness before God. (Isai. 64:6)

6. **Removing Filthy Garments:** (v. 4) The act of removing the filthy garments from Joshua represents the forgiveness of sins and the cleansing of impurity. It is an act of divine grace and mercy.

7. **Pure Vestments and Clean Turban:** (v. 5) Joshua is then clothed in pure, clean vestments. This symbolizes the righteousness and holiness that God imparts to His people through His redemptive work. The clean turban on Joshua's head is a sign of his restored priestly position and his renewed relationship with God. It represents the acceptance and favor of God.

8. **Double Imputation** (vv. 4, 5) These passages bear similarities to the concept of double imputation in Christian theology.

    1) Sin Imputed to Christ: The filthy garments symbolize the sin and unrighteousness of Joshua. The angel's actions symbolize Christ's redemptive work. He intervenes to remove the filthy garments, signifying the imputation of sin on Christ through His sacrifice.

    2) Righteousness Imputed to Believers: Joshua is then clothed in clean garments, symbolizing the imputation of righteousness through God's grace. This parallels the imputation of Christ's righteousness to believers.

In summary, Zechariah 3:1–5 portrays a powerful image of God's mercy, redemption, and the restoration of a sinful people through Christ's intervention. The passage foreshadows the gospel message of forgiveness, cleansing, and the imputation of Christ's righteousness to believers. It emphasizes God's desire to cleanse His people and restore them despite their shortcomings and challenges.

65. PROPHET ISAIAH

The conversion of Isaiah is a significant event described in the book of Isaiah. It is a powerful encounter that profoundly impacted the life and ministry of the prophet Isaiah. The account of Isaiah's conversion is found in Isaiah 6:1–8 and provides insight into his transformation and calling to prophetic service. It describes the prophet Isaiah's encounter with God and his response to that encounter.

1. **His Conviction of sin:** (vv. 1–4) Isaiah sees a vision of the Lord seated on a throne, high and exalted. The imagery and grandeur of the vision highlight God's holiness and glory. This revelation of God's holiness brings about a deep awareness of Isaiah's own sinfulness. The Holy Spirit is the sole agent of the conviction of sins (John 16:8).

2. **His Contrition of sin:** (v. 5a) After witnessing the divine presence and holiness, Isaiah becomes overwhelmed with a sense of his own unworthiness. He exclaims, "Woe is me! For I am undone! Isaiah realizes his sinfulness in the presence of the holy God and expresses deep remorse. (Ps. 51:17)

3. **His Confession of sin:** (v. 5b) Isaiah acknowledges his sinful state, particularly focusing on his unclean lips. By saying, "Because I am a man of unclean lips, and I dwell in the midst of a people of unclean lips, for my eyes have seen the King, the Lord of hosts!" he recognizes that his words and speech have not been aligned with God's holiness. This confession demonstrates Isaiah's humility and recognition of his need for forgiveness. (Rom. 10:9)

4. **His Conversion:** (vv. 6-7 NIV) a seraph flies to Isaiah with a burning coal from the altar and touches his mouth with it, saying, "Behold, this has touched your lips; your iniquity is taken away, and your sin purged." This act symbolizes the purification and forgiveness of Isaiah's sin. Through this cleansing, Isaiah experiences a transformation and restoration, with his iniquity removed and his sins purged. (Matt. 18:3)

5. **His Consecration:** (v. 8) after being cleansed and forgiven, Isaiah responds to God's call. He hears the voice of the Lord saying, "Whom shall I send? And who will go for Us?" Isaiah then willingly offers himself, saying, "Here am I. Send me!" This shows his readiness to serve God and his commitment to being a messenger of God's words to the people. (Rom. 12:1-2)

The conversion of Isaiah serves as a powerful example of God's transformative work in the lives of His chosen servants. Isaiah's encounter with the holiness of God leads to a deep awareness of his own sinfulness and the sin of his people. Yet, in the midst of this revelation, Isaiah experiences the mercy and forgiveness of God, which enables him to respond to God's call with humility and obedience. Isaiah's conversion highlights the crucial elements of true repentance and surrender to God's will. It reminds us that encountering God's holiness should lead us to acknowledge our need for His grace and forgiveness. Like Isaiah, we are called to respond to God's call and be willing vessels for His purposes. Throughout his prophetic ministry, Isaiah faithfully proclaimed God's message, confronted injustice, and foretold the coming of the Messiah. His conversion experience became the foundation of his prophetic authority and his unwavering commitment to fulfill the mission entrusted to him. The conversion of Isaiah stands as a timeless reminder that God can transform lives and use imperfect individuals to accomplish His divine plans. It encourages us to seek God's presence, repent of our sins, and willingly respond to His call, knowing that He equips and empowers those who surrender to Him.

66. SALVATION MADE PLAIN AND SIMPLE

Isaiah 45:22, a profound verse in the Bible, encapsulates the simplicity, source, security, and scope of salvation. Within these lines, we find the essence of redemption offered to humanity through divine grace. Each segment sheds light on different aspects of this timeless truth, inviting all to embrace the promise of salvation.

1. **The Simplicity** of Salvation: "Look"
   In the simplicity of a single word, the prophet Isaiah beckons humanity to turn its gaze towards the source of eternal hope. "Look," he declares, stripping away all complexities, offering a straightforward path to salvation. A child can look. One who is almost an idiot can look. If he looks, the promise is that he shall live. Sometimes, salvation is so simple that people stumble all over it. They have a hard time believing that it can be so simple. (John 1:29)

The Assurance of Salvation

2. **The Source** of Salvation: "Me"
   In this declaration, the divine speaker asserts His exclusive role as the source of salvation. "Me," He declares, emphasizing that redemption flows solely from His divine being, reinforcing the intimacy of the relationship between the Creator and His creation. Salvation can be found only in Him. There is but one way to escape from Hell, and that is through God's plan of salvation. Salvation comes through Jesus Christ alone. "For I am God, and there is no other." (Acts 4:12)

3. **The Security** of Salvation: "be saved"
   Within these two words lies the assurance of eternal security. "Be saved," the promise echoes, assuring that those who heed the call will find deliverance from the bondage of sin and the certainty of eternal life. When a person looks to Jesus Christ for salvation, that person is saved from the penalty of sin. Real salvation is absolute and eternal deliverance from sin and death. When Jesus saves a lost soul, He does it eternally. (Rom. 6:23b)

4. **The Scope** of Salvation: "All you ends of the earth"
   Expanding the horizon of redemption, Isaiah's words transcend boundaries and reach out to the farthest corners of the earth. "All you ends of the earth," the invitation resounds, inclusive and universal, extending the offer of salvation to every nation, tribe, and tongue. One of the truths about God's plan of salvation that makes it so great is the fact that it is for every individual in the whole world. It is not offered to a select few, but to "whosoever will." (John 3:16)

The salvation of God extends an invitation that is both universal and personal, inviting all to gaze upon the divine source of redemption, find security in His promise, and embrace the boundless scope of His grace. May this truth continue to resonate in the hearts of all who hear it, guiding them towards the hope and assurance found in the embrace of divine love.

67. THE ROMAN ROAD MAP

The Romans road map for salvation aims to present a condensed summary of key theological concepts from the book of Romans in the Bible, which highlights the universal problem of sin, the redemptive work of Jesus

EXAMINE SCRIPTURE RELATED TO SALVATION

Christ, and the free gift of salvation through faith in Him. Let's go through each point:

1. **You are a sinner** (3:23): This verse highlights the Christian belief that all human beings are sinners. It states, "For all have sinned and fall short of the glory of God." It acknowledges that every individual has fallen short of God's perfect standard and has committed acts that are contrary to His will.

2. **You cannot save yourself** (3:20 NIV): It states, "Therefore no one will be declared righteous in God's sight by the works of the law; rather, through the law we become conscious of our sin." It highlights the inability of human efforts or good works to save oneself and attain righteousness before God. This phrase emphasizes the consequence of sin. Sin leads to spiritual death and separation from God. It implies that sin carries a penalty, and that penalty is death.

3. **The wages of sin is death** (6:23a): It says, "For the wages of sin is death." It emphasizes that sin carries a penalty, which is spiritual and eternal death, meaning separation from God. This verse points out the inability of human beings to save themselves from the consequences of sin. It highlights the futility of relying on personal efforts, good works, or religious rituals alone to achieve salvation. The message is that no one can earn salvation by their own merit.

4. **Christ died for you** (5:8): It states, "But God demonstrates his own love towards us, in that while we were still sinners, Christ died for us." This verse highlights the sacrificial death of Jesus Christ on the cross as an expression of God's love for humanity. It emphasizes that Jesus Christ, the Son of God, willingly sacrificed Himself by dying on the cross to pay the penalty for humanity's sins. Jesus's death provides a way for individuals to be reconciled with God and receive salvation.

5. **The gift of God is eternal life** (6:23b): It states, "But the gift of God is eternal life in Christ Jesus our Lord." It emphasizes that eternal life, which is a restored relationship with God and salvation, is a gift freely given by God through Jesus Christ. In the Christian faith, it is believed that humans are separated from God because of sin, but through Jesus

Christ, God offers the gift of eternal life. This gift is not earned or deserved; it is freely given by God's grace.

6. **You need to confess with your mouth** (10:9): This refers to Romans 10:9, which says, "That if you confess with your mouth the Lord Jesus and believe in your heart that God has raised Him from the dead, you will be saved." It emphasizes the importance of confessing and believing in Jesus Christ as Lord and Savior. Confession and belief are essential elements of the Christian faith and serve as a way to express faith and surrender to Jesus as Lord and Savior.

7. **Nothing can separate you from the love of Christ** (8:35): This verse, Romans 8:35, states, "Who shall separate us from the love of Christ? Shall tribulation, or distress, or persecution, or famine, or nakedness, or peril, or sword?" It reassures believers that no circumstance or challenge can separate them from the love of Christ. It emphasizes the unbreakable and unconditional love that Jesus has for His followers. Regardless of hardships, trials, or any other challenges, the love of Christ remains constant and steadfast.

In summary, these statements from the book of Romans in the Bible outline the Christian understanding of salvation. They acknowledge human sinfulness, the consequence of sin, the inability of humans to save themselves, and the belief in Jesus's sacrificial death as the means of salvation.

68. A JUSTIFIED CRIMINAL

In Luke 23:39–43, we encounter a fascinating and touching narrative that delves into the concept of redemption and forgiveness, even in the darkest of circumstances. The passage centers around three individuals crucified alongside Jesus Christ on the day of His crucifixion. Among them is a justified criminal, whose life story holds profound lessons about the power of faith and the promise of salvation. In this brief exploration, we shall unravel the essence of the justified criminal's encounter with Jesus and how it serves as a timeless reminder of hope, grace, and the transformative nature of true repentance.

EXAMINE SCRIPTURE RELATED TO SALVATION

1. **The Similarities of the Two Criminals**

    1) The same race   (Jews)
    2) The same religion   (Judaism)
    3) The same character   (notorious)
    4) The same occupation   (thieves, robbers)
    5) The same party   (Zealot partisans)
    6) The same place of death (Calvary)

2. **Their Differences**

    1) The criminal who received Jesus Christ was saved (justified)
    2) The criminal who rejected Jesus Christ was lost (condemned)

3. **Three Crosses at Calvary**

    1) The Cross of Jesus Christ (the cross of redemption)
    2) The cross of the saved criminal (the cross of reception)
    3) The cross of the lost criminal (the cross of rejection)

4. **"The Four Best" in one particular verse Luke 23:43**

    1) "Assuredly" (the best promise)
    2) "Today" (the best time)
    3) "Me" (Jesus, the best Friend)
    4) "Paradise" (the best place)

5. **Three Different Status at Calvary**

1	Lord Jesus Christ	No Sin in Him	Sin on Him	Our Savior
2	The Saved Criminal	Sin in him	No sin on him	Paradise
3	The Lost Criminal	Sin in him	Sin on him	Hell

6. **Christ, the Great Divider** (Luke 23:39–43)

    1) Only Two Groups of People: Here, we find a profound illustration of the division that Christ brings among people, evident in the

contrasting responses of the two criminals crucified alongside Him. This passage reveals that there are ultimately only two groups of people in the world, and where each individual stands in relation to Christ determines their eternal destiny.

2) The Lost Criminal: The scene unfolds with the whole world represented by these two criminals. One of them joins the crowd of those who reject Christ. His words and actions demonstrate a heart closed to the message of salvation. He scoffs at Jesus, demanding that He save both of them if He truly is the Christ. This criminal, though facing imminent judgment and death, remains blinded to the truth and unwilling to recognize the Savior before him.

3) The Saved Criminal: On the other side stands the saved criminal, a striking contrast to his counterpart. Despite sharing the same fate of crucifixion, his response sets him apart from the rest of the world. He acknowledges his own sinfulness and the just punishment he deserves, openly confessing that their suffering is warranted, but Jesus is innocent. In a humble and desperate plea, he turns to Christ, recognizing His divinity and authority, asking to be remembered in His kingdom.

4) Reject or Receive: Jesus's response to this humble request is one of profound grace and compassion. He assures the saved criminal that he will be with Him in paradise that very day. Here, we witness the power of salvation and the redemption that comes from placing faith in Christ alone. The saved criminal's repentance and belief in Jesus result in the promise of eternal life, exemplifying the truth that Christ is the Great Divider between those who receive Him and those who reject Him.

5) Where Do You Stand Right Now? This passage calls us to examine where we stand today. Are we like the saved criminal, acknowledging our need for a Savior and placing our trust in Jesus's finished work on the cross? Or are we like the lost criminal, hardened in heart and refusing the free gift of salvation offered by Christ?

6) **You Need to Receive Him by Repentance and Faith:** Dear friends, the message of Luke 23:39–43 is as relevant today as it was during those historical events. Christ continues to be the Great Divider among humanity, and our response to Him determines our eternal destiny. Let us not delay but come to Christ with humility, repentance, and faith, receiving His forgiveness and the assurance of everlasting life. May we stand with the saved criminal, firmly rooted in the hope of Christ's redemptive love, and experience the joy of being remembered in His eternal kingdom.

7) **Guarantee for Paradise:** The story of the justified criminal serves as an inspiring testament to the boundless mercy and love of Jesus Christ. Despite his life of wrongdoing and facing the consequences of his actions on the cross, the justified criminal found salvation at the eleventh hour through a simple yet profound expression of faith. Jesus's response to him not only granted him forgiveness but also guaranteed his eternal place in paradise.

This biblical account speaks to the core of Christianity—no matter how dire our circumstances or grievous our sins, we are never beyond redemption. The justified criminal's journey from despair to hope, from condemnation to salvation, offers a powerful message of encouragement and reassurance to all who seek forgiveness and transformation. It emphasizes the significance of genuine repentance and the readiness of Jesus to extend grace to those who turn to Him with a contrite heart. As we reflect on the story of the justified criminal, let us remember that we, too, have the opportunity to embrace the gift of salvation through faith in Jesus Christ. May it inspire us to live lives characterized by compassion, love, and a willingness to extend forgiveness to others, just as our Savior has done for us. Ultimately, the tale of the justified criminal is a reminder of the extraordinary and life-changing power of Christ's sacrificial love for humanity.

69. THE HOLY COMMUNION

The Lord's Supper, also known as the Holy Communion or the Eucharist, is a sacrament observed by many Christian denominations as a commemoration of the Last Supper of Jesus Christ with his disciples. It is mentioned in the New Testament of the Bible, specifically in 1 Corinthians

11:23–34. This passage provides us with important details about the significance and proper observance of the Lord's Supper. The cup of wine symbolizes the blood of Jesus Christ, which provides the remission of sins for believers, bringing spiritual healing. The broken bread represents the stripes on Christ's body, signifying our physical healing.

1. **Upward Look - Christ's body and blood** (vv. 23–25): In this section, the apostle Paul recounts the words of Jesus during the Last Supper. He emphasizes that the bread represents Christ's body, and the cup represents His blood, which was shed for the forgiveness of sins. The act of partaking in the bread and wine symbolizes our connection with Christ and the spiritual nourishment we receive through His sacrifice.

2. **Backward Look - His death at the cross** (v. 26): By participating in the Lord's Supper, Christians are reminded of Jesus's death on the cross, His sacrificial act that reconciled humanity with God. This backward look helps believers reflect on the significance of Christ's sacrifice and the grace they have received through His death.

3. **Forward Look - His second coming** (v. 26): The Lord's Supper is not only a remembrance of Christ's past sacrifice but also a forward-looking anticipation of His second coming. Christians partake in the sacrament with the expectation of Christ's return and the establishment of His kingdom. It serves as a reminder of the hope and future glory that believers have in Christ.

4. **Inward Look - unworthy manner** (vv. 27–29): In these verses, Paul warns the Corinthians about partaking in the Lord's Supper in an unworthy manner. He urges them to examine themselves and confess and repent of any unconfessed sins before participating. This inward look reminds believers of the need for personal introspection, repentance, and a genuine faith in Christ. Self-examination involves acknowledging and affirming the presence of Christ within us through the Holy Spirit (2 Cor. 13:5).

5. **Outward Look - to love and care for others** (vv. 30–34): The final aspect highlights the importance of the outward look. Paul points out that some of the Corinthians were not showing proper regard for their

fellow poor believers during the Lord's Supper, leading to divisions and mistreatment of one another. He exhorts them to love and care for one another, treating each other with dignity and respect. The Lord's Supper should be a time of unity and fellowship among believers.

From the perspective that Holy Communion is primarily for thanksgiving rather than salvation, the focus is on expressing gratitude for the sacrifice of Jesus on the cross. The bread and wine symbolize his body and blood, representing the ultimate act of love and self-sacrifice that resulted in salvation. The act of participating in Holy Communion is seen as a way to remember and reflect upon the sacrificial death of Jesus and give thanks for the forgiveness of sins and the salvation that Christians believe comes through faith in him. This thanksgiving is directed toward God for the gift of salvation and the eternal life believers have in Christ. Overall, the perspective that Holy Communion is primarily for thanksgiving aligns with the idea that it is a way for believers to remember and honor the sacrifice of Jesus Christ, expressing gratitude for the salvation that his sacrifice provides.

70. CONCLUSION

In conclusion, the passage from 1 John 5:12–13 encapsulates a profound assurance of salvation that resonates through the ages. By affirming that the one who possesses the Son possesses life, the passage emphasizes the inseparable bond between faith in Christ and the eternal life that follows. This assurance is not based on fleeting emotions or circumstances but is grounded in the unchanging promise of God's grace and the redemptive work of Jesus.

The apostle John's words offer comfort and certainty to believers, reminding them that they can have confidence in their relationship with God and their eternal destiny. This assurance does not lead to complacency but rather serves as a catalyst for a life transformed by love, obedience, and devotion to God. As John writes, these things have been written so that believers may know they have eternal life, spurring them on to live with purpose and conviction.

In a world marked by uncertainty, the assurance of salvation provided in these verses serves as an anchor for the soul, enabling believers to navigate life's challenges with a steadfast faith. It is a reminder that the gift of eternal life is not earned but received through faith in Christ. This assurance also fosters a sense of unity among believers, as they share in the common hope of salvation.

The most crucial distinctive about Christianity is that in Christianity, people can truly have genuine assurance of salvation. They can be certain that they are going to heaven because their salvation is anchored in what Jesus already did for them. As a result, Christians have peace in their hearts about where they will go when their lives on earth are finished.

In other faiths, people cannot be assured that they will go to heaven because they can never know if they have done enough good works to earn God's favor or forgiveness. They have to continually try to earn their salvation—even until their last day and dying breath. They cannot experience the restful assurance that God gives those who trust in Jesus Christ.

Ultimately, the passage encourages a deepening relationship with God, built upon the foundation of Christ's sacrifice and the indwelling of the Holy Spirit. It beckons believers to approach God with boldness, knowing their salvation is secure and that they are loved beyond measure. As we meditate on these verses, may we be inspired to live lives that reflect the profound truth of our assurance in Christ, impacting the world around us and glorifying the One who has granted us eternal life.

PRAYER FOR SALVATION

Prayer for the salvation of those who have not been born again is important because it aligns with God's desire for all people to come to faith in Jesus Christ. It acknowledges our dependence on God's work and invites His intervention in the lives of unbelievers. While prayer does not guarantee salvation, it can create an atmosphere conducive to spiritual openness and prepare the way for the Holy Spirit to work in a person's heart.

1. **Prayer for Individuals** (2 Cor. 4:3-4)
   "And even if our gospel is veiled, it is veiled to those who are perishing. In their case the god of this world has blinded the minds of the unbelievers, to keep them from seeing the light of the gospel of the glory of Christ, who is the image of God." This passage highlights the spiritual

blindness that afflicts those who have not accepted the message of the gospel. Regarding the importance of prayer for the salvation of unbelievers, it is crucial to understand that prayer plays a significant role in the life of a Christian. Prayer is a means of communicating with God, expressing our desires, seeking His guidance, and interceding for others. Christians are encouraged to pray for all people, including those who have not yet embraced the salvation offered through faith in Jesus Christ. Through prayer, Christians can ask God to open the hearts and minds of unbelievers, remove spiritual blindness, and bring them into a saving relationship with Jesus Christ. Prayer also acknowledges our dependence on God's work in the process of salvation and invites Him to intervene in the lives of those who have not been born again. Salvation ultimately depends on a person's response to the gospel and their personal relationship with God. Prayer can create an atmosphere of spiritual openness and prepare the way for the Holy Spirit to work in the lives of unbelievers.

> **Prayer is an act of love.** It is true that our love for unsaved family members, for non-Christian friends, for unreached peoples can drive us to prayer. But ultimately, prayer is the domain of God, and it is impossible to be passionate about prayer if you are not already passionate for Him. Our engagement in faithful, overcoming intercession for the salvation of all peoples and the redemption of the world can be sustained only by a deep and unshakeable love for our Lord. After all, it is for His glory that we long to see the world changed through prayer. (Mandryk 2010, xxiv)[29]

2. **Prayer for Children** (4/14 Window)
   The "4/14 Window" refers to a specific age range, from four to fourteen years old. This concept highlights the idea that children between these ages are particularly receptive to spiritual and moral formation. It is believed that during this period of childhood, children are more open to spiritual truths and are more likely to accept and integrate faith-based values into their lives. Therefore, there is a significant emphasis on reaching and evangelizing children within this age group, with the hope of shaping their beliefs and values early in life. The goal is to foster

a lifelong commitment to Christianity and to help them grow as committed followers of Jesus.

3. **Prayer for Other Faiths** (10/40 Window)
The "10/40 Window" refers to a specific geographical area on the world map. It spans from ten degrees to forty degrees latitude north of the equator and encompasses parts of Africa, the Middle East, and Asia. This region is often referred to as the "resistant belt" because it includes many countries where Christianity is a minority religion and where there may be cultural, religious, or political barriers to the spread of Christianity. Additionally, the 10/40 Window is home to a large percentage of the world's population, as well as many of the world's least-reached and least-evangelized people groups. Christians have focused their prayer and mission efforts on the 10/40 Window because it contains a significant number of unreached people groups and individuals who have limited access to the message of Christianity. The goal of this emphasis is to bring the message of Jesus Christ to those who have not yet heard the gospel.

MY INVITATION

In the journey of life, we are often faced with numerous decisions that shape our present and future. Some decisions hold more significance than others, carrying the weight of eternity. One such decision is whether to receive the salvation offered through Jesus Christ before it is too late. The concept of salvation holds a profound meaning for those who believe, as it offers the promise of forgiveness, redemption, and eternal life. However, the urgency lies in the fact that the opportunity to make this decision may not last forever. Therefore, it becomes crucial to carefully consider and embrace the message of salvation, recognizing its transformative power and the eternal implications it holds.

1. **All Will Not Be Saved** (Matt. 13:30): Jesus tells the parable of the wheat and the tares, explaining that at the end of the age, the wheat (representing the righteous) will be separated from the tares (representing the wicked). This suggests that not everyone will be saved. There is no such thing as universal salvation; some will be saved, and

others will be lost. There are only two groups of people in this world, the saved and the lost. Will you be among the saved or among the lost?

2. **The Majority Will Be Lost** (Matt. 7:13–14): Jesus speaks about the narrow gate and the wide gate. He emphasizes that the way leading to eternal life is narrow and difficult, and only a few will find it, while the way that leads to destruction is broad, and many will enter through it. This suggests that the majority will not be saved. It was at the time of Noah and the flood when only eight were saved. All others perished. Do you remember Sodom and Gomorrah? Only three escaped.

3. **Many Will Perish Who Expect to Be Saved** (Matt. 7:21–23): Jesus warns about those who claim to know Him and do mighty works in His name but are not truly converted in Christ. He declares that He will say to them, "I never knew you; depart from me, you who practice lawlessness." This indicates that there will be people who believe they are saved but will ultimately be lost. Profession without possession, and the door of mercy is closed and lost forever.

4. **There Is No Salvation after Death** (Heb. 9:27): It is stated that "And as it is appointed for men to die once, but after this the judgment." This verse suggests that there is no opportunity for salvation after death. It emphasizes the importance of seeking salvation during one's earthly life, as the afterlife is a time of judgment rather than a chance for redemption. Each person will be held accountable for their actions and faith during their lifetime. We do not believe in life circles or purgatory.

5. **This May Be Your Last Opportunity** (Acts 24:25): It recounts an encounter between the apostle Paul and Felix, the governor of Judea. It is mentioned that Paul reasoned with Felix about "faith in Christ Jesus," which suggests that Felix had an opportunity to hear the gospel. The verse serves as a reminder that opportunities to encounter the gospel and accept salvation should not be taken lightly, as we do not know when our last chance to respond may come.

6. **When the Harvest Is Past** (Jer. 8:20): "The harvest is past, the summer is ended, and we are not saved." This verse speaks to the urgency of seeking salvation and turning to God before it is too late. It emphasizes

the importance of recognizing the need for redemption and seeking it in a timely manner. There are times when God's Spirit is actively at work in a community, when the gospel is being preached and souls are being saved. To miss such opportunities is to run the risk of being lost and lost eternally.

7. **You Need to Accept Christ Right Now** (2 Cor. 6:2): It emphasizes the urgency of responding to God's grace and accepting Jesus as one's Savior. Paul is urging the Corinthians not to delay or procrastinate in accepting the salvation offered by God. This verse is often used to emphasize the importance of making a decision to follow Jesus without delay, as it suggests that the time of God's favor and salvation is now. It encourages people to recognize the urgency of the matter and not put off their decision to accept Jesus.

It is an invitation to embrace a life-changing relationship with the Creator, experiencing forgiveness, restoration, and eternal joy. The urgency lies in the uncertainty of time, as none of us can predict the length of our days. Procrastination or indifference toward this decision may lead to missed opportunities and regrets in the eternal future. Embracing salvation in Christ allows us to walk in the light of truth, love, and purpose, in this life and the next. May we approach this decision with open hearts, seeking wisdom and responding to the call of salvation before it is too late.

MY TESTIMONY

1. How I Came to Know Jesus Christ

I was raised in a Baptist family in Northern Chin State, where attending Sunday School regularly was part of my upbringing as I sought to become a better Christian. At the age of 17, I was baptized by our pastor. However, at that time, I had little understanding of the true path to salvation. The baptismal training I received placed a strong emphasis on good works. We believed that baptism washed away all sins, and I was under the impression that if I died right after being baptized, I would surely go to heaven. In response, I tried my best to live righteously, avoiding wrongdoing. I abstained from alcohol, smoking, and theft, and I faithfully gave my tithes.

Additionally, I was a regular churchgoer and a dedicated choir member, all in hopes of securing my salvation.

While working as a high school teacher, I was transferred from Hakha to Paletwa, a region in southern Chin State known for its prevalence of malaria. I later learned that 17 missionaries from the West had lost their lives to malaria in that area. Upon arriving at Sittwe airport, the capital of Rakhine, a doctor advised me to begin taking quinine immediately. The sight of so many people succumbing to malaria deeply unsettled me and led me to question, "Where will I spend eternity?" Unable to answer this, I became deeply troubled about the state of my salvation. My thoughts wandered to the differences between living beings: trees, which possess only a body, animals, which have a body and soul but lack a spirit, and humans, who have a body, soul, and spirit. These reflections left me so disturbed that I could neither eat nor sleep for several days.

An evangelist came from afar and preached about Christ, who "takes away the sin of the world." Although I understood this intellectually, I didn't feel it in my heart. The next day was incredibly challenging for me. On the night of December 9, 1975, I couldn't sleep, lying awake in bed. I prayed to God, surrendering everything from the depths of my heart. Suddenly, I had a vision of my Savior, Jesus Christ, hanging on the cross. He spoke to my heart, assuring me that He had taken away all my sins and cleansed me with His blood. In that moment, I felt a warm sensation as He entered my heart. Filled with indescribable joy, I began to cry like a baby. I had never experienced such profound happiness before.

The next morning, I got up early and went to greet my neighbors, exclaiming, "My sins have been forgiven!" They looked at me in astonishment. After being born again, everything around me seemed new and beautiful—the animals, my unruly students, even the scenery. At the time, I was teaching English to 9th graders and matriculation classes. I couldn't stop smiling, my heart filled with happiness, and my students noticed my joyful spirit. Following my conversion, I was so full of joy that I didn't eat or sleep for four days and nights. Yet, I didn't feel hungry or tired. I was intensely aware of Jesus' presence within me. As a newborn in faith, I was concerned that my Lord, who was dwelling within me, might suffer from hunger or lack of rest. However, one morning, I heard a sermon on the Far East Broadcasting

Service that said, "God neither slumbers nor sleeps" (Ps. 121:4). From that moment, I stopped worrying about my Lord suffering because of me.

2. I Am Sure I Have Eternal Life

After being born again and knowing that all my sins had been forgiven, I was deeply troubled when a senior told me that forgiveness of sin was not enough for salvation; one also needed to know they had eternal life. This statement shook my peace of mind and assurance of salvation, leaving me in great confusion. On December 12, three days after being born again, I asked God to reveal in a dream whether I had eternal life.

In my dream, I saw my Savior Jesus Christ and His Father sitting on chairs beside a big table. I appeared as a kindergarten student with a shoulder bag. Regarding my concern about eternal life, my Lord Jesus said I was like a KG student who, having registered on the first day of school, asked every day whether his name was on the list. Then, Jesus and His Father laughed at me lovingly. I cannot forget the way they looked at me and their loving faces. From that moment on, I have had the assurance of eternal life and have not doubted it since.

ABOUT THE AUTHOR

I am Cin Thang graduated from Rangoon University in 1968. Born again in Paletwa, Chin State in 1975. In 1980, he left his teaching job and joined the Union Biblical Seminary in Yavatmal, India under the Serampore Senate in 1980-83. His ministry journey began in the Siyin Region Baptist Association and within the Zomi Baptist Convention, he played a pivotal role as a resource person in various areas, such as evangelism and missions (Chins for Christ in One Century), youth, and women's conferences. He later pursued further studies, earning a Doctor of Ministry degree from Union Theological Seminary (Philippines), jointly with Myanmar Institute of Theology, in 2007. He served as the senior pastor at Yangon Siyin Baptist Church from 1992 to 2009. He also held the position of principal at All Nations Theological Seminary from 2001 to 2020, contributing to the education and training of future religious leaders. Additionally, he remained active as a resource person in the Evangelism and Mission Department of the Myanmar Baptist Convention from 1992 to 2022. Various language and regional groups across the country frequently invited him to share the gospel.

BIBLIOGRAPHY

Berkhof, Louis. *Manual of Christian Doctrine*. Grand Rapids: Wm. B. Eerdmans Publishing Com., 1933.

Bird, Michael F. *Evangelical Theology: A Biblical and Systematic Introduction*. 2nd ed. Grand Rapids: Zondervan, 2020.

Carter, Tom. *2200 Quotations from Writings of Charles H. Spurgeon*. Grand Rapids: Baker Books, 1988.

Day, Millard F. *Basic Bible Doctrines*. Chicago: Moody Press, 1953.

Enns, Paul. *The Moody Handbook of Theology*. Chicago: Moody Publishers, 2008.

Grudem, Wayne. *Systematic Theology: An Introduction to Biblical Doctrine*. Grand Rapids: Zondervan, 1994.

Grudem, Wayne. *Bible Doctrine: Essential Teachings of the Christian Faith*. 2nd ed. London: InterVarsity Press, 2022.

Harwood, Adam. *Christian Theology*. Bellingham: Lexham Press, 2022.

Jeffress, Robert. *Not All Roads Lead to Heaven*. Grand Rapids: Baker Books, 2016.

Knight, George, W. *Pocket Bible Dictionary*. Uhrichsville: Barbour Publishing, 1998.

Lewis, Gordon R, and Demarest, Bruce A. *Integrative Theology: Historical, Biblical, Systematic, Apologetic, Practical: Three Volumes in One*. Grand Rapids: Zondervan, 1996.

Luther, Martin. n.d. "Martin Luther Quotes, On Christian Liberty." *Good Reads*. Accessed January 4, 2024. https://www.goodreads.com/quotes/735033-good-works-do-not-make-a-good-man-but-a

MacArthur, John. *The MacArthur Bible Commentary*. Nashville: Thomas Nelson, 2005.

Mandryk, Jason. *Operation World 7th. Edition*. Downers Grove: Inter Varsity Press, 2010.

Metzger, Bruce M, and Coogan, Michael D. *The Oxford Companion to The Bible*. New York: Oxford University Press, 1993.

Moo, Douglas J. *The NIV Application Commentary 2 Peter, Jude*. Grand Rapids: Zondervan, 1996.

Stott, John. *The Cross of Christ*. London: InterVarsity Press, 2021.

Thang, Lam Cin. *Ketinchin Seikchiah Hmuh*. Yangon: Myanmar Baptist Press, 2022.

Unger, Merrill F. *The new Unger's Bible Dictionary*. Chicago: Moody Publishers, 1988.

Wijaya, Philip. "What is the Difference Between Grace and Mercy?". *Christianity*. Last modified July 23, 2023. https://www.christianity.com/wiki/christian-terms/what-is-the-difference-between-grace-and-mercy.html

ENDNOTES AND CITATION WITH NUMBERS

1. Grudem, Wayne. *Bible Doctrine: Essential Teachings of the Christian Faith.* 2nd ed. London: InterVarsity Press, 2022

2. Grudem, Wayne. *Systematic Theology: An Introduction to Biblical Doctrine.* Grand Rapids: Zondervan, 1994.

3. Unger, Merrill F. *The new Unger's Bible Dictionary.* Chicago: Moody Publishers, 1988.

4. Stott, John. *The Cross of Christ.* London: InterVarsity Press, 2021.

5. Unger, Merrill F. *The new Unger's Bible Dictionary.* Chicago: Moody Publishers, 1988.

6. Grudem, Wayne. *Bible Doctrine: Essential Teachings of the Christian Faith.* 2nd ed. London: InterVarsity Press, 2022.

7. Harwood, Adam. *Christian Theology.* Bellingham: Lexham Press, 2022.

8. Enns, Paul. *The Moody Handbook of Theology.* Chicago: Moody Publishers, 2008.

9. Lewis, Gordon R, and Demarest, Bruce A. *Integrative Theology: Historical, Biblical, Systematic, Apologetic, Practical: Three Volumes in One.* Grand Rapids: Zondervan, 1996.

10. Berkhof, Louis. *Manual of Christian Doctrine.* Grand Rapids: Wm.B.Eerdmans Publishing Com, 1933.

11. Grudem, Wayne. *Bible Doctrine: Essential Teachings of the Christian Faith.* 2nd ed. London: InterVarsity Press, 2022.

12. Knight, George W. *Pocket Bible Dictionary.* Uhrichsville: Barbour Publishing, 1998.

13 Bird, Michael F. *Evangelical Theology: A Biblical and Systematic Introduction.* 2nd ed. Grand Rapids: Zondervan, 2020.

14 Bird, Michael F. *Evangelical Theology: A Biblical and Systematic Introduction.* 2nd ed. Grand Rapids: Zondervan, 2020.

15 Bird, Michael F. *Evangelical Theology: A Biblical and Systematic Introduction.* 2nd ed. Grand Rapids: Zondervan, 2020.

16 Thang, Lam Cin. *Ketinchin Seikchiah Hmuh.* Yangon: Myanmar Baptist Press, 2022.

17 Thang, Lam Cin. *Ketinchin Seikchiah Hmuh.* Yangon: Myanmar Baptist Press, 2022.

18 Thang, Lam Cin. *Ketinchin Seikchiah Hmuh.* Yangon: Myanmar Baptist Press, 2022.

19 Day, Millard F. *Basic Bible Doctrines.* Chicago: Moody Press, 1953.

20 Carter, Tom. *2200 Quotations from Writings of Charles H. Spurgeon.* Grand Rapids: Baker Books, 1988.

21 Jeffress, Robert. *Not All Roads Lead to Heaven.* Grand Rapids: Baker Books, 2016.

22 Luther, Martin. n.d. "Martin Luther Quotes, On Christian Liberty." *Good Reads.* Accessed January 4, 2024. https://www.goodreads.com/quotes/735033-good-works-do-not-make-a-good-man-but-a

23 Wijaya, Philip. "What is the Difference Between Grace and Mercy?". *Christianity.* Last modified July 23, 2023. https://www.christianity.com/wiki/christian-terms/what-is-the-difference-between-grace-and-mercy.html

24 MacArthur, John. *The MacArthur Bible Commentary.* Nashville: Thomas Nelson, 2005.

25 Metzger, Bruce M, and Coogan, Michael D. *The Oxford Companion to The Bible.* New York: Oxford University Press, 1993.

26 Moo, Douglas J. *The NIV Application Commentary 2 Peter, Jude.* Grand Rapids: Zondervan, 1996.

27 Unger, Merrill F. *The new Unger's Bible Dictionary.* Chicago: Moody Publishers, 1988.

28 Unger, Merrill F. *The new Unger's Bible Dictionary*. Chicago: Moody Publishers, 1988.

29 Mandryk, Jason. *Operation World 7th. Edition*. Downers Grove: Inter Varsity Press, 2010.